The New York Times

Large Type cook book

The New York Times

Large Type cook book

BY **JEAN HEWITT**

ILLUSTRATIONS BY **MAIDA SILVERMAN**

GOLDEN PRESS  **NEW YORK**

This book is dedicated with affection to Craig Claiborne,

The New York Times Food Editor,

a respected and admired colleague,

with gratitude for the opportunities, encouragement and invaluable help

he has so generously given over the years.

Foreword

A collection of specially selected recipes in clear, bold type can aid, encourage and, I believe, inspire all cooks to greater triumphs.

The inexperienced and the neophyte in the kitchen will follow the recipes with a new degree of assurance...the ¼ teaspoon of "that" and the ⅛ teaspoon of "this" will not be accidentally transposed as the eye flits from page to pan and back again. For those with impaired vision the benefits are immediately apparent. For those who wear glasses for reading, but not for actual cooking processes, it offers freedom from the distracting "on and off" routine. The experienced cook will follow the easy-to-read type with extra confidence and be encouraged to experiment with new recipes.

6

The New York Times Large Type Cookbook can be read from a considerable distance by the majority, making it possible to check an ingredient, refer to a procedure or prepare for the next step while still stirring at the stove or counting out eggs at the refrigerator.

The book offers a general collection of *Times*-tested recipes, ranging from the simple to the exotic and touching on many of the world's cuisines. Carefully selected, they are the best recipes from among the thousands that have appeared in the pages of *The New York Times* during the past two years. There are variations on classic recipes, a number of old favorites and original ideas from many different sources.

There is a tremendous back-to-the-kitchen movement in progress that represents more than a need-to-eat instinct and coincides with fast-diminishing sources of household help. I am confident that the movement can be nurtured by the easy-to-read, simple but elegant recipes in this book.

Without the many friends and people who have contributed recipes, and ideas for recipes, that have appeared in *The New York Times*, this book would not have been possible. My thanks go to Mrs. Velma Cannon and Miss Anita Rizzi of the Food News staff for their untiring assistance, cheerfully given. Last, but not least, my gratitude goes to my family, Eric, Gordon and Geoffrey, for their patience and understanding during the preparation of the manuscript.

JEAN HEWITT

Contents

Appetizers

Guacamole

Yield: About 3 cups

2 ripe avocados, peeled and
    finely chopped

1 tomato, skinned and
    chopped

1 tablespoon finely
    chopped onion

1 clove garlic, finely
    chopped

2 tablespoons lemon or
    lime juice

1 tablespoon chopped
    green chili peppers

1½ teaspoons salt

¼ teaspoon black pepper

¼ teaspoon cayenne pepper

1 teaspoon chopped fresh
    coriander leaves
    (available in Spanish
    and Chinese markets)

Mix all ingredients in an electric blender just before serving, as the mixture darkens if held for any time. For a smoother texture, mixture may be blended in 2 or 3 batches.

Note: Two mushrooms, thinly sliced or chopped, may be added before serving.

Salmon Sour Cream Dip

Yield: About 1 pint

1 can (1 pound) salmon

½ teaspoon salt

4 drops Tabasco sauce,
  or to taste

1 teaspoon grated onion

1 cup sour cream

1 tablespoon drained red
  caviar

Fresh vegetable dippers

1. Drain and flake the fish. Blend in salt, Tabasco and onion. Fold in sour cream and chill.

2. Garnish with caviar. Serve with vegetable dippers (cauliflowerets, celery, carrot, green pepper and cucumber sticks) which have been chilled until crisp.

Laban

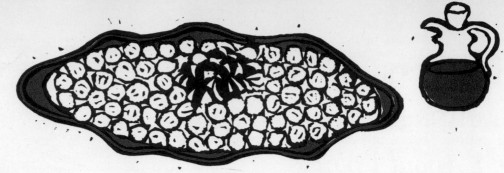

Yield: About 1½ cups or 6 servings

4 cups plain yogurt	2 tablespoons chopped
½ teaspoon salt	fresh mint leaves
⅓ cup olive oil	Mint leaves

1. Mix yogurt and salt and put in a cheesecloth bag made with several layers of cloth. Tie bag and suspend over a bowl to catch drips; leave overnight at room temperature.

2. Remove solid cheeselike mixture from bag and either form into balls or into a mound with a depression in the middle. Place in a serving dish. Pour olive oil over balls or into depression; sprinkle with chopped mint. Garnish with whole mint leaves.

Chicken Liver- Champagne Pâté

Yield: 6 servings

1 pound chicken livers	3 tablespoons bacon fat
2 tablespoons flour	¼ pound mushrooms,
Salt and black pepper	sliced
2 cloves garlic, finely	½ cup (approximately)
chopped	champagne

1. Dredge chicken livers in flour seasoned with salt and pepper.

2. Sauté garlic in bacon fat 2 minutes. Turn up heat, add chicken livers and cook 3 minutes, turning. Add mushrooms and cook 1 minute longer. Check seasonings.

3. Turn liver mixture into the container of electric blender. Add champagne slowly, while blending until mixture is smooth and of suitable consistency. Scrape into a small crock and chill well before serving with toast triangles.

15

Chicken Pâté Loaf

Yield: 12 servings

2 tablespoons butter
1 whole chicken breast, split in half, skinned and boned
½ pound chicken livers
2 shallots, chopped
½ pound mushrooms, sliced
¼ cup warm cognac
1 cup chicken broth

½ teaspoon salt
¼ teaspoon black pepper
1 envelope unflavored gelatin
¼ cup water
¼ cup mayonnaise
½ cup heavy cream
Stuffed olives
Truffles
Parsley

1. Melt butter in a heavy skillet and brown chicken breast on both sides, a total of about 4 minutes.

2. Add livers and cook quickly 2 minutes, browning on all sides. Lower heat slightly; add shallots and mushrooms and cook 2 minutes, stirring twice.

16

3. Pour warm cognac over chicken; stand back and ignite.

4. When flame subsides, add broth, salt and pepper. Bring to a boil and simmer 1 minute or until chicken is tender.

5. Remove chicken, dice and reserve. Strain broth from livers and measure 1¼ cups. Evaporate by boiling if too much or add water if not enough.

6. Place gelatin in an electric blender, add water and blend on low speed until gelatin softens. Heat ¾ cup of reserved broth to a boil; pour into blender and blend on low speed until gelatin dissolves.

7. Add remaining broth, mayonnaise and cream. Turn blender to high speed, add liver mixture and blend until smooth. Fold in diced chicken and turn into a lightly oiled 4-cup mold. Chill at least 4 hours before unmolding. Garnish with stuffed olives, truffles and parsley. Serve with thin toast.

Note: The chicken may be added along with chicken livers and blended smooth if desired.

17

Marinated Salmon

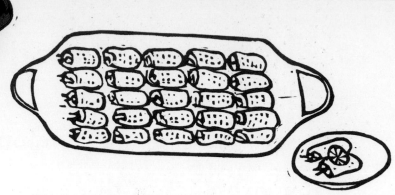

Yield: 12 servings

3 pounds fresh salmon

½ cup chopped green
  pepper

½ cup chopped pimento

1 cup lime juice

1½ cups beer

½ cup imported soy sauce

1 tablespoon finely
  chopped fresh ginger
  or ½ teaspoon ground

1 clove garlic, mashed

2 tablespoons grated onion

1. Skin salmon and remove bones. Cutting diagonally across grain, slice salmon into thin strips, 3 to 4 inches long.

2. Spread salmon, green pepper and pimento in a thin layer in shallow pan. Cover fish with lime juice and 1 cup beer. Refrigerate several hours, until opaque and pink.

3. Drain fish. Rinse with cold water; drain. Lay pieces flat. Place a little marinated pepper and pimento at one end of each piece of salmon and roll. Fasten with toothpicks.

4. Mix soy sauce with the remaining beer, ginger, garlic and onion. Use as dip with salmon.

Tuna-Stuffed Eggs

Yield: 12 servings

12 hard-cooked eggs
1 can (7 ounces) solid
   white tuna
½ cup mayonnaise
¼ teaspoon salt
⅛ teaspoon black pepper

2 tablespoons Madeira or
   cognac
⅛ teaspoon thyme
⅓ cup chopped pecans
1 tablespoon chopped parsley
   Pimento cutouts
   Capers

1. Halve eggs lengthwise; scoop yolks into a bowl and mash.

2. Add remaining ingredients except pimento and capers to yolks and mix well.

3. Fill egg whites with mixture. Garnish with pimento and capers. Chill.

Egg and Endive

Yield: 12 to 16 appetizers

3 hard-cooked eggs
2 tablespoons crumbled
    Roquefort or blue
    cheese
2 tablespoons (approxi-
    mately) mayonnaise

Salt and black pepper
¼ teaspoon Tabasco sauce
2 or 3 Belgian endives
6 to 8 flat anchovy fillets,
    cut in half lengthwise
Chopped parsley

1. Shell eggs and chop well. Place in mixing bowl and add cheese and mayonnaise. Stir and, if necessary, add more mayonnaise to bind mixture. Season to taste with salt, pepper and Tabasco.
2. Pull apart endive leaves. Spread egg mixture inside endive leaves and lay half an anchovy fillet lengthwise over each. Garnish with chopped parsley. Chill and serve.

Crab-Stuffed Tomatoes

Yield: 20 servings

20 small cherry tomatoes

1 cup mayonnaise

¼ cup finely chopped
  shallots or scallions

2 tablespoons chopped chives

2 teaspoons tarragon

1 tablespoon chopped
  parsley

1 teaspoon thyme

2 tablespoons basil

1 tablespoon finely
  minced garlic

1 hard-cooked egg, finely
  sieved

1 pound lump crab meat

Salt and black pepper
  to taste

1. Pare away core of each tomato, leaving a cavity for the crab filling. Salt inside of tomatoes and turn them upside down to drain.

2. Combine remaining ingredients and use to fill centers of tomatoes. Garnish with parsley sprigs and serve cold.

21

Cheese Crisps

Yield: About 4 dozen squares

1 cup flour	½ cup butter, at room
Salt	temperature
¼ teaspoon cayenne pepper	¼ cup milk or cream
⅔ cup freshly grated	
Parmesan cheese	

1. Preheat oven to 350 degrees.

2. Place flour in a mixing bowl and add salt, cayenne and cheese.

3. Add butter and work dough with the fingers until it just holds together. Gather dough into a ball and roll out on a lightly floured board to ⅛-inch thickness. Brush dough lightly with milk or cream and slice it into 1-inch squares. With a spatula, transfer the squares to a baking dish.

4. Bake 12 to 15 minutes or until lightly browned.

Cocktail Wafers

Yield: About 40 biscuits

⅔ cup sesame seeds

2 cups flour

1 teaspoon salt

¼ teaspoon cayenne pepper

¾ cup butter

3 to 4 tablespoons cold water

1. Preheat oven to 300 degrees.

2. Place sesame seeds on a baking sheet and bake until light brown. Meanwhile, prepare dough.

3. Place flour in a mixing bowl and add salt and cayenne. Using pastry blender, cut in butter until mixture has consistency of coarse cornmeal. Add seeds. Toss mixture with a 2-pronged fork, adding just enough water so that dough holds together and has the consistency of biscuit dough.

4. Roll dough on a lightly floured board. Roll almost as thin as pie crust, about ⅛ inch thick. Cut into rounds with very small biscuit cutter. Arrange rounds on baking sheet and bake 15 to 20 minutes. Sprinkle hot biscuits with salt.

23

Gefilte Fish Crescents

Yield: 32 crescents

1½ cups flour

½ teaspoon salt

½ cup kosher-pareve
   margarine

4 to 5 tablespoons ice
   water

1 jar (15½ ounces)
   unsalted gefilte fish

1½ tablespoons lemon juice

1 tablespoon finely minced
   shallot

½ teaspoon tarragon

1 egg, lightly beaten

1. Sift flour and salt into a bowl. Cut in margarine until particles are very fine. Add enough ice water to make a dough. Work into a ball and chill.

2. Preheat oven to 400 degrees.

3. Drain fish and place in a bowl. Mash very well and add lemon juice, shallot and tarragon. Mix. Divide in half.

4. Divide pastry in half. Roll out one half into 10-inch circle. Spread half the fish mixture over entire surface, making sure it is even.

5. Cut into 16 wedges with a sharp knife. Beginning at outside edge, roll each wedge tightly to form a crescent. Arrange on lightly greased baking sheet and brush rolls with beaten egg.

6. Repeat with remaining pastry and fish mixture. Bake about 20 minutes or until lightly browned. Serve hot.

Briks

Yield: 12 to 18 briks

2 cups flour

⅛ teaspoon salt

8 egg yolks

⅓ cup (approximately)
water

1 can (7 ounces) tuna

2 tablespoons capers

Oil for deep-frying

1. Mix flour and salt and place on a board. Make a depression in center. Put 2 egg yolks and some of the water into hole. Gradually mix flour and liquid with the fingers to make a pliable but dry dough, adding water as needed.

2. Let ball of dough rest at least 15 minutes, covered with a damp towel.

3. Meanwhile, flake the undrained tuna and mix in remaining egg yolks and capers.

4. Roll out dough until it is very thin, like noodle dough. Cut into 2- or 3-inch squares or rounds.

26

5. Place a tablespoon of tuna mixture in middle of each piece of dough. Moisten edges with some of the egg white and fold squares to make triangles, fold rounds to make crescents. Seal edges.

6. Fry pastries two or three at a time in deep oil heated to 365 degrees until golden on all sides. Remove with a slotted spoon and drain on paper towels. Serve warm.

Chicken Liver Strudel Slices

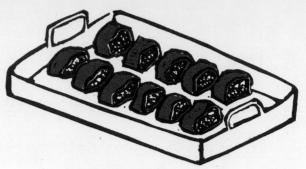

Yield: 18 to 24 slices

1 onion, finely chopped
6 tablespoons butter
1 pound chicken livers
¼ pound mushrooms, sliced
2 tablespoons cognac
¼ cup soft bread crumbs
Salt and black pepper

1 egg, lightly beaten
⅛ teaspoon allspice
2 tablespoons chopped
 parsley
¼ pound (approximately)
 phyllo pastry
Melted butter

1. In a small skillet, sauté onion in 2 tablespoons butter until tender but not browned.

2. Add remaining butter and livers. Cook quickly until browned on all sides. Add mushrooms and cook 3 minutes longer.

3. Turn liver mixture onto a chopping board and chop until fine. Scrape into a bowl and add cognac, bread crumbs, salt, pepper, eggs, allspice and parsley. Mix. Allow to cool.

4. Preheat oven to 375 degrees.

5. Place 2 sheets of phyllo pastry on damp cloth; brush with melted butter. Top with 2 more sheets of pastry; brush with butter and top with 2 more sheets. More sheets of pastry, up to a total of 10, may be used if desired.

6. Mold liver mixture into a sausage shape along longest side of pastry and roll like a jelly roll. Lift carefully and place, seam side down, on a baking sheet, preferably one with low sides in case fat oozes out while baking.

7. Bake until pastry is crisp and golden, 30 to 40 minutes. Serve immediately.

8. If making ahead of time, cool. Chill and wrap in aluminum foil or set in a foil dish and cover to freeze.

9. Remove from freezer ½ hour before serving. Preheat oven to 375 degrees.

10. After 10 to 15 minutes' thawing, the roll can be cut into ½-inch slices and set upright or on sides on a baking sheet. Bake 15 minutes or until heated through.

Individual Shrimp Quiches

Yield: 2 to 3 dozen, depending on size of pans

½ cup soft butter

4 ounces cream cheese

2 tablespoons heavy cream

1¼ cups flour

½ teaspoon salt

1½ to 2 cups roughly cut, cooked, shelled and deveined shrimp (see note)

1½ cups heavy cream

3 eggs, lightly beaten

¼ cup finely grated Gruyère or Swiss cheese

Salt and black pepper to taste

1 teaspoon snipped fresh dill

⅓ cup freshly grated Parmesan cheese

1. Cream butter and cream cheese very well. Beat in 2 tablespoons cream and then work in flour and salt to make a dough. Wrap in wax paper and refrigerate several hours or overnight.

2. Preheat oven to 425 degrees.

3. Roll out pastry to ⅛-inch thickness and cut into rounds to fit very small, one-bite-size, muffin tins. Fit rounds into tins.

4. Distribute shrimp in pastry cases. Combine cream, eggs, Gruyère, salt, pepper and dill. Spoon mixture over shrimp.

5. Sprinkle tops of tarts with Parmesan and bake 5 minutes. Reduce oven temperature to 350 degrees and bake 15 minutes longer, or until quiches are set and lightly browned on top. Serve immediately.

6. If making ahead of time, cool on rack. Chill. Pack in boxes lined with foil or aluminum dishes; cover with foil, freeze. Remove from freezer about ½ hour before serving.

7. Preheat oven to 375 degrees. Place quiches on a baking sheet and bake 15 to 20 minutes or until heated through.

Note: The shrimp can be replaced by other shellfish, mushrooms, chopped ham or bacon and sautéed onions. If filling is not shellfish, the dill should be replaced by ⅛ teaspoon nutmeg.

Crab Meat Appetizers

Yield: 6 servings

½ pound lump crab meat

2 tablespoons butter

2 tablespoons flour

¾ cup milk

  Salt and black pepper

  Tabasco sauce to taste

1 teaspoon lemon juice

½ teaspoon Worcestershire
    sauce

1 tablespoon chopped
    chives

6 slices white bread

12 flat anchovy fillets

¼ cup fresh bread crumbs

¼ cup freshly grated
    Parmesan cheese

Parsley sprigs

6 thin slices lemon

1. Preheat oven to 400 degrees.

2. Pick over crab meat.

3. Melt butter in a saucepan and stir in flour. Add milk, stirring rapidly with a wire whisk. Season to taste with salt and pepper and simmer about 5 minutes. Stir in crab and add Tabasco, lemon juice, Worcestershire and chives.

4. Trim crusts off bread and cut into triangles. Broil lightly on both sides.

5. Spread crab mixture over each triangle and top with an anchovy fillet. Sprinkle with a mixture of bread crumbs and cheese and place on a baking sheet. Place in oven just to heat through.

6. Garnish with parsley and ½ slice of lemon. Serve hot.

Cocktail Meat Balls

Yield: 3 to 4 dozen cocktail-size meat balls

1 pound ground round beef

½ pound sausage meat

1 small onion, finely grated

2 slices bread

Cold water

Salt and black pepper
   to taste

1 tablespoon chopped
   green pepper

1 tablespoon chopped capers

½ teaspoon thyme

1 tablespoon chopped
   parsley

1 egg, lightly beaten

Salad oil

2 cups homemade tomato
   sauce (page 247)

1. Mix together beef, sausage, onion, bread soaked in water and squeezed dry, salt, pepper, green pepper, capers, thyme and parsley. Mix in egg.

2. Form mixture into 36 to 48 half-inch balls.

3. Pour into a large heavy skillet a tablespoon of oil or just enough to grease the bottom.

4. Heat oil and add single layer of meat balls. Sauté, turning frequently, until browned on all sides and cooked.

5. Drain meat balls; add to hot tomato sauce and serve.

6. If making ahead of time, cool, chill and pack in a plastic bag for freezing. The tomato sauce can be held for weeks in the refrigerator or freezer.

7. Remove meat balls from freezer about 1 hour before serving. Heat tomato sauce in a large saucepan and place meat balls in sauce. Place over very low heat, stirring occasionally, until heated through. Serve in a fondue pot or chafing dish with bamboo skewers.

Miniature Drumsticks

Yield: 18 servings

3 pounds broiler-fryer
  chicken wings (about 18)
½ cup flour
½ cup freshly grated
  Parmesan cheese
1 teaspoon monosodium
  glutamate

1 teaspoon salt
1 teaspoon paprika
½ teaspoon oregano
¼ teaspoon Tabasco sauce
¾ cup buttermilk
Oil for deep-frying

1. Cut the wings in half and use the "drumstick" half for frying.

2. Blend flour, cheese, monosodium glutamate, salt, paprika and oregano. Add Tabasco to buttermilk.

3. Dip chicken "drumsticks" in buttermilk; shake to remove excess. Roll in dry ingredients.

4. Cook chicken pieces about 5 minutes in deep oil heated to 365 degrees.

Angels on Horseback

Yield: 24 appetizers

24 plump raw oysters

¼ cup lemon juice

3 dashes Tabasco sauce

1 teaspoon Worcestershire

½ teaspoon salt

12 strips bacon

1. Preheat oven to 450 degrees.

2. Drain oysters on absorbent toweling.

3. Place oysters in a mixing bowl and add lemon juice, Tabasco, Worcestershire and salt. Stir briefly to coat oysters with sauce.

4. Cut each bacon strip in half and use each half to wrap an oyster. Secure with toothpicks and place on a rack in baking dish. Bake until bacon is crisp.

Tuna-Stuffed Mushrooms

Yield: 8 to 10 servings

1 pound large mushrooms	1 tablespoon capers
2 teaspoons lemon juice	1 can (7 ounces)
1½ teaspoons chopped	tuna in oil, flaked
onion	2 to 3 tablespoons
⅛ teaspoon black pepper	freshly grated
3 tablespoons mayonnaise	Parmesan cheese

1. Preheat oven to 350 degrees.

2. Rinse and dry mushrooms. Break off stems and discard or use in a soup or sauce. Mix lemon juice, onion, pepper and mayonnaise. Add capers and tuna and spoon into mushroom cups.

3. Sprinkle with cheese. Place in a greased baking pan and bake until hot, about 20 minutes.

Seviche

Yield: 6 or more servings

2 cups fish fillets, cut into
   ½-inch cubes (see note)

½ cup chopped onion

2 small hot green peppers,
   finely chopped, or
   Tabasco sauce to taste

⅓ cup fresh lime juice

½ cup tomato juice

⅓ cup olive oil

1 large tomato, chopped

1½ cloves garlic, minced

½ teaspoon thyme
   Salt and black pepper

1 tablespoon chopped
   parsley

1 tablespoon chopped
   fresh coriander
   leaves (optional)

¼ cup finely chopped
   sweet red peppers

It is essential to the success of this dish that the fish be as fresh as possible. Combine all ingredients and let stand in the refrigerator overnight. (The lime juice "cooks" the fish.)

Note: You can use flounder, red snapper, bass or scallops.

Sea Food Canapés

Yield: 6 servings

6 Holland rusks

6 tablespoons cream cheese

6 thick slices tomato

3 hard-cooked eggs, halved
   lengthwise

   Salt and black pepper

1 pound cooked, shelled
   and deveined
   shrimp or picked-over
   crab meat

1 cup homemade
   mayonnaise (page 244)

½ cup catchup

1 teaspoon lemon juice

1 teaspoon Worcestershire
   sauce

1 tablespoon anchovy paste

2 teaspoons grated onion

   Tabasco sauce to taste

¼ cup chopped fresh chives
   or parsley

1. Spread each rusk with a tablespoon of cream cheese. Top
   with a slice of tomato.
2. Place an egg half, cut side down, in center of each tomato
   slice and sprinkle with salt and pepper. Arrange shrimp or
   crab meat around egg half.

3. Combine remaining ingredients except chives and blend well. Spoon over the canapés. Garnish each with chopped chives or parsley.

Tomato and Anchovy Canapés

Yield: 6 servings

6 slices trimmed toast
18 thin slices tomato
12 flat anchovy fillets
½ clove garlic, minced
3 tablespoons wine vinegar
Salt and black pepper

9 tablespoons olive oil
1 hard-cooked egg, chopped
2 tablespoons finely chopped parsley

1. Arrange toast on 6 small plates. Top each slice with 3 tomato slices. Garnish each serving with 2 crossed anchovies.

2. Place garlic in a mixing bowl and add remaining ingredients. Stir to blend and pour over canapés.

41

Ham Cornets

Yield: 12 servings

12 slices baked Virginia ham, cut about ⅛ inch thick (1 to 1½ pounds)

¾ cup homemade aspic or canned jellied con-sommé, partly jelled

1 tablespoon butter

2 shallots, finely minced

4 mushrooms, chopped

1 tablespoon flour

⅓ cup light or heavy cream

2 cups ground cooked ham

1 tablespoon tomato paste

1 tablespoon snipped fresh dill

1 tablespoon cognac

Black pepper

Truffle cutouts

2 cups potato or Russian (diced vegetable) salad

Watercress sprigs

1. Form a cone with each slice of ham. Dip into aspic or jellied consommé and secure with toothpicks or place in metal molds used in making pastry cones. Chill.

42

2. Melt butter in small skillet and sauté shallots until tender. Add mushrooms and cook until liquid has evaporated.

3. Sprinkle with flour; cook 1 minute. Stir in cream and cook until mixture thickens; simmer 1 minute.

4. Combine mushroom mixture, ground ham, tomato paste, dill, cognac and ¼ cup of the partly jelled aspic. Season to taste with pepper.

5. Remove ham cones from molds and spoon in the stuffing. Brush all over with remaining aspic and decorate the end with truffle cutouts. Chill. Arrange cones on a mound of potato or Russian salad. Garnish with watercress.

Dolmadakia

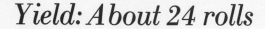

Yield: About 24 rolls

1 cup olive oil

3 large onions, chopped

1 clove garlic, finely
    chopped

1 teaspoon salt

¼ teaspoon black pepper

1 cup rice

2 tablespoons snipped
    fresh dill

¼ cup finely chopped
    Italian parsley

2 tablespoons pine nuts

6 scallions, finely chopped

1 cup lemon juice

3 cups water

1 jar (8 ounces) grape
    leaves

Lemon wedges

1. Heat ½ cup oil in a skillet and sauté onion and garlic until tender.

2. Add salt, pepper and rice and cook slowly 10 minutes, stirring frequently. Add dill, parsley, nuts, scallions, ½ cup lemon juice and 1 cup water; stir. Cover and simmer gently until liquid has been absorbed, about 15 minutes.

3. Rinse grape leaves under running water, separate and place shiny side down on a board. If leaves are small, put two together.

4. Place 1 teaspoon rice filling near stem end of each leaf and roll up jelly-roll fashion toward tip, tucking in edges to make a neat roll.

5. Place remaining oil, lemon juice and 1 cup water in a large skillet. Arrange rolls in pan, separating layers with parsley stems if more than one layer is made. Place a heavy plate over or plate and weight on top and simmer 25 minutes. Add 1 cup water and cook about 10 minutes longer. Cool. Serve with lemon wedges.

Crab Vinaigrette

Yield: 6 to 8 servings

3 tablespoons finely
   chopped scallions
1 tablespoon chopped
   fresh tarragon
1 tablespoon chopped
   parsley
1 tablespoon capers
½ teaspoon chopped garlic
½ teaspoon Dijon mustard

Salt and black pepper
¼ cup lemon or lime juice
½ cup peanut oil
2 teaspoons chopped
   anchovies
1 hard-cooked egg, sieved
1 teaspoon paprika
1 pound lump crab meat,
   picked over

1. Mix all ingredients except crab meat.

2. Put 2 tablespoons sauce in a skillet and add crab. Toss gently and heat through. Add remaining sauce. Heat to lukewarm. Spoon mixture into individual crab shells or ramekins. Serve warm with wedges of lemon and buttered toast.

Baked Oysters

Yield: 6 to 8 servings

6 cloves garlic, minced

10 scallions, finely chopped

1½ cups chopped parsley

1 tablespoon olive oil

1 quart medium-size
    shucked oysters

Black pepper

Juice of 2 lemons

1 cup dry white wine

2 tablespoons Worcester-
    shire sauce

4 tablespoons butter

2 tablespoons flour

1. Preheat oven to 350 degrees.

2. Combine garlic, scallions and parsley. Toss well.

3. Pour olive oil into bottom of a 1½-quart casserole. Add a layer of the herb mixture and a layer of oysters; sprinkle with pepper. Continue making alternate layers.

4. Pour over all lemon juice, wine and Worcestershire. Dot with butter. Sift flour gently over the casserole to prevent lumping. Bake 35 minutes. Serve with pumpernickel.

Creamed Oysters
in Barquettes

Yield: 20 servings

Pastry:
 2 cups flour
 1 teaspoon sugar
 ½ teaspoon salt
 ⅓ cup butter
 ⅓ cup shortening
 Ice water

Filling:
 6 tablespoons butter
 6 tablespoons flour
 2½ pints oysters, drained
  and juice reserved

2½ cups, approximately,
  heavy cream (light
  cream or milk may be
  substituted)
1 tablespoon lemon juice,
  or to taste
¼ cup dry sherry
 Salt and cayenne pepper
  to taste
 Parsley sprigs

1. Several hours or a day ahead, make pastry cases. Preheat oven to 425 degrees.

48

2. Place flour, sugar and salt in a bowl. With fingertips or a pastry blender, blend in butter and shortening.

3. Mixing with a fork, add just enough ice water to make a dough, about 3 tablespoons. Roll out dough on a lightly floured board or pastry cloth to ⅛-inch thickness. Cut 20 ovals to fit barquette pans or rounds to fit small tartelette pans. Chill.

4. Prick once with fork and bake 10 minutes, until done and lightly browned. Cool.

5. Shortly before serving, make filling. Melt butter in a heavy pan and blend in flour. Measure oyster liquid and make up to 3½ cups with cream or milk.

6. Gradually blend the liquid into butter and flour. Bring to a boil, stirring constantly, and cook 2 to 3 minutes. The sauce can be held over hot water for up to an hour.

7. Add oysters and cook until edges just curl, about 2 minutes. Add lemon juice, sherry, salt and cayenne; immediately serve in the pastry shells. Garnish with parsley.

Shrimp Tarragon

Yield: 4 servings

5 tablespoons butter	½ teaspoon tarragon
36 medium-size shrimp, shelled and deveined	Black pepper to taste
	1 teaspoon lemon juice
Salt to taste	3 tablespoons warm cognac
2 tablespoons finely minced shallots	¾ cup heavy cream, heated
	1 tablespoon flour

1. Melt 4 tablespoons butter in a chafing dish and, when hot, add shrimp in one layer. Sprinkle with salt. Cook shrimp until pink on both sides, turning, about 4 minutes.

2. Sprinkle shrimp with shallots, tarragon, pepper and lemon juice and continue cooking, stirring. Sprinkle with warm cognac; ignite. Spoon sauce over shrimp as flame burns.

3. Pour cream over shrimp; bring to boil. Whisk in flour blended with remaining butter. Cook, stirring, until thickened. Serve immediately.

Soups

Caldo Gallego
(Spanish Soup with Greens)

Yield: 3 quarts

½ pound dried chick-peas
    or white marrow beans
¼ pound lean salt pork,
    diced
¼ cup cooked smoked ham,
    diced
¼ pound chorizos (Spanish
    sausages), sliced
2 tomatoes, skinned and
    chopped
2 cloves garlic, finely chopped

1 ham bone
2 quarts water
1½ teaspoons cumin
    Salt and black pepper
    to taste
4 small potatoes, peeled
    and diced
½ pound dandelion greens
    or spinach

1. If chick-peas are used, cover with water, bring to a boil and drain. If white beans are used, cover with water, soak overnight and then drain.

52

2. Sauté salt pork until lightly browned; add the ham and sausage and cook until lightly browned.

3. Add peas or beans, tomato, garlic, ham bone, water, cumin, salt and pepper to salt pork. Cover and bring to a boil; simmer about 1½ hours or until peas or beans are tender.

4. Meanwhile, wash greens and cut into large pieces. Cook in a little butter until wilted; set aside.

5. Add potatoes and cook 20 minutes longer. Add greens and cook 5 minutes longer. Remove bone; correct seasoning.

Borscht

Yield: 6 to 12 servings

2 marrow bones	2 large tomatoes, skinned
2 knuckle bones	Salt to taste
1 brisket of beef	1 white cabbage
(3 pounds)	10 to 12 fresh beets
1 large onion, peeled	1 tablespoon sugar
3 sprigs parsley	1 tablespoon vinegar
3 large sprigs dill	2 or more crystals sour salt
Pinch of thyme	(citric acid crystals)
2 bay leaves	2 cups sour cream
12 peppercorns	6 to 12 freshly boiled
2 carrots, quartered	potatoes, peeled

1. Place marrow and knuckle bones in a large kettle and cover with water. Bring to a boil and simmer about 1 minute. Drain and rinse bones under cold running water. Return bones to kettle.

54

2. Add beef and onion to kettle; add water to cover. Place kettle over moderate heat.

3. Add parsley, dill, thyme, bay leaves and peppercorns tied in a muslin bag. Add carrots, tomatoes and salt. Bring to a boil and partly cover. Total cooking time for the brisket will be about 3 hours. Skim surface frequently as brisket cooks.

4. After brisket has cooked 2 hours, prepare the cabbage. Coarsely shred cabbage and add boiling water to cover. Drain and add cabbage to kettle.

5. When brisket is tender, remove and reserve to be served as boiled beef.

6. Continue with borscht. Peel beets; slice them and add to kettle. Cook until beets are thoroughly tender, 30 minutes to 1 hour. When done, remove and discard bones and muslin bag. Add sugar, vinegar, sour salt and salt to taste. The flavor should be sweet and sour. Serve soup with sour cream and potatoes.

Green Borscht

Yield: About 2 quarts

3 to 4 pounds lean boned
  beef shank, chuck or
  California roast
2 quarts cold water
  Salt and black pepper
  to taste
1 carrot, diced
1 parsnip, diced
1 large leek, chopped
4 ribs celery

½ pound sorrel leaves
  (sour grass), chopped
½ pound spinach leaves,
  chopped
4 small potatoes, peeled
  and diced
Sugar
4 hard-cooked eggs,
  quartered
Sour cream

1. Place meat in a deep heavy kettle. Add the water. Bring to
   a boil. Add salt, pepper, carrot, parsnip, leek and celery;
   cover and simmer until meat is tender, 1 to 1½ hours.

2. Add sorrel, spinach and potatoes and continue to cook,
   covered, until the potatoes are tender, about 20 minutes.

3. Remove meat, cut into bite-size pieces and return to kettle. Taste for seasoning; if too sour, add 1 or 2 teaspoons sugar. Add eggs. Spoon sour cream onto each serving.

Egg Drop Soup

Yield: 4 servings

3 cups chicken broth
½ teaspoon monosodium glutamate
2 teaspoons cornstarch
2 tablespoons cold water

1 scallion, trimmed and cut into ¼-inch pieces
1 egg, well beaten
Pepper (preferably white)

1. Bring chicken broth to a boil. If broth is freshly made, add monosodium glutamate; if broth is canned, omit.

2. Blend cornstarch with water and add slowly to broth, stirring. When broth is thickened, add scallion pieces.

3. Stirring the soup rapidly, gradually add beaten egg. Remove from heat immediately and season with pepper.

Vegetable and Rice Soup

Yield: 6 or more servings

6 tablespoons butter

4 leeks, trimmed, split in half, washed well and chopped

2 cups cubed white turnips

1 cup chopped celery

½ cup chopped onion

½ teaspoon chopped garlic

3 medium-size tomatoes, skinned and quartered

2 cups beef broth

2 cups water

1 cucumber, peeled and sliced

Salt and black pepper

¼ cup uncooked rice

¾ cup heavy cream

1. Melt half the butter in a saucepan and cook leeks, stirring frequently, until golden brown. Add turnips, celery, onion, garlic, tomatoes, beef broth, water and cucumber. Add salt and pepper and bring to a boil. Simmer 1 hour. Strain through a fine sieve or blend.

2. Return soup to the saucepan and add rice. Simmer 30 minutes. Add cream; bring just to a boil. Remove soup from heat and swirl in remaining butter.

Onion Soup

Yield: 6 servings

¼ cup butter

4 large onions, thinly sliced

4 cups beef stock

¼ teaspoon pepper

Salt to taste

1 teaspoon lemon juice

6 slices toasted French bread

6 tablespoons freshly grated Parmesan cheese

1. Heat butter in a large saucepan and cook onions over low heat until tender, stirring to separate onion into rings.

2. Add stock and pepper and bring to a boil. Add salt and lemon juice and keep hot. To serve, place a slice of toast on each serving and sprinkle with 1 tablespoon cheese.

59

Olive-Bean Soup

Yield: 6 servings

 1 cup dried white beans
 5 whole cloves
 5 whole peppercorns
 5 whole allspice
 1 ham hock
 1 large onion, chopped

 1 clove garlic, finely chopped
 1 teaspoon salt
 ½ cup ripe olives, cut into
   wedges
 2 tablespoons chopped parsley

1. Cover beans with water and soak overnight.

2. Drain beans and place in a kettle with 1½ quarts water and the cloves, peppercorns and allspice tied in a muslin bag.

3. Add ham hock, onion, garlic and salt. Bring to a boil, cover and simmer until the beans are tender, about 1½ hours. Remove bag.

4. Remove ham from bone; dice meat, return it to kettle with olives and reheat. Mash a few of the beans to give body to the soup. Sprinkle with parsley.

Pea Soup

Yield: 12 to 16 servings

1 pound dried green or
   yellow peas
1 beef shank bone
2 ribs celery with leaves
1 onion, studded with
   4 cloves
2 carrots, quartered

Salt to taste
10 peppercorns
1 bay leaf
2 ribs celery, chopped
2 carrots, diced or sliced
1 small ham bone
¼ teaspoon rosemary

1. Cover peas with water and soak overnight.

2. Place shank bone in a large kettle and cover with water. Bring to a boil; drain and cover with 1 gallon of water. Add whole celery ribs, onion, quartered carrots, salt, peppercorns and bay leaf. Cover; simmer 2 hours. Strain liquid into another kettle.

3. Drain peas and add with remaining ingredients. Simmer, covered, about 1 hour. Remove bone. Check seasoning.

Cream of Watercress Soup

Yield: 8 servings

1 bunch watercress

6 tablespoons butter

1 cup chopped onion

4 medium potatoes, peeled and quartered (about 3 cups)

2 cups chicken broth

2 cups water

Salt and black pepper

1 cup heavy cream

1. Rinse watercress. Shred about 20 leaves without stems and set aside. Clean remaining leaves; cut off tough stems.

2. Heat 4 tablespoons butter in a large saucepan and cook onion until wilted. Add leaves and potatoes. Add chicken broth and water and cook until potatoes are tender.

3. Put soup through a sieve; season with salt and pepper and stir in cream. Bring to a boil. Remove from heat and add shredded leaves and remaining butter.

Curried Eggplant Soup

Yield: 4 servings

1 tablespoon olive oil	2 teaspoons curry powder
1 cup cubed unpeeled eggplant	2 cups milk
¼ cup minced onion	¼ teaspoon crushed oregano
½ teaspoon minced garlic	¼ teaspoon crushed rosemary
1 tablespoon butter	Salt and black pepper
4 teaspoons flour	½ cup heavy cream

1. Heat oil in a skillet and cook eggplant until golden brown.

2. In a saucepan, cook onion and garlic in butter until onion is wilted. Sprinkle with flour and curry powder, stirring with a whisk until blended. Add milk, stirring rapidly. When mixture is thick, add seasonings and eggplant and simmer 15 minutes.

3. Puree mixture; return to a boil and add cream. Serve hot.

Celery Chowder

Yield: 8 to 10 servings

¼ pound salt pork, diced
3 onions, thinly sliced
1 quart milk
3 large potatoes, peeled and diced

3 cups celery, diagonally sliced into small pieces
2 tablespoons flour
Salt and black pepper

1. Sauté salt pork in a heavy kettle until crisp and brown. Remove pork pieces and reserve.

2. Sauté onions in pork fat remaining in kettle until tender but not browned.

3. Heat all but ¼ cup milk to boiling; add to kettle with potatoes and celery. Bring to a boil; cover and simmer about 20 minutes or until potatoes are tender.

4. Blend flour with remaining milk. Add a little of the hot soup and mix; return to pan and cook, stirring, until soup thickens. Add salt and pepper; sprinkle with salt pork.

Corn Chowder

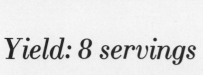

Yield: 8 servings

½ pound salt pork, diced
¼ cup chopped onion
½ cup chopped celery
¼ cup chopped green pepper
1 cup diced raw potatoes
2 cups water
2 teaspoons turmeric
½ bay leaf

Salt and black pepper
3 tablespoons flour
2 cups milk
2 cups freshly cut corn kernels (about 4 large ears)
2 tablespoons chopped parsley

1. Sauté salt pork until crisp and golden. Add onion and celery; cook until tender but not browned. Add green pepper, potatoes, water, turmeric, bay leaf, salt and pepper. Simmer 20 minutes, until potatoes are barely tender.
2. Mix flour with ½ cup milk. Heat remaining milk and add to blended flour. Stir into hot soup and heat, stirring until mixture thickens. Add corn and parsley.
3. Cook about 4 minutes. Check seasoning.

Old-Fashioned Clam Chowder

Yield: 15 to 20 servings (about 5 quarts)

5 to 6 dozen chowder clams

½ pound salt pork, diced

6 large onions, sliced

4 to 6 leeks, trimmed, washed and sliced

3 tomatoes, skinned and chopped

2 cups canned tomatoes

3 ribs celery, diced

1 tablespoon chopped parsley

1 teaspoon thyme

1 bay leaf

3 large potatoes, peeled and diced

Salt and black pepper

2 tablespoons flour

2 tablespoons butter

2 Pilot biscuits, crumbled

1 teaspoon Worcestershire sauce

2 to 4 drops Tabasco sauce

1. Scrub clams until water runs clear and place in a large kettle or clam steamer with ½ cup water. Steam clams until they open, about 10 minutes, depending on size.

2. Save the liquid. Remove clams from shells and discard long necks and coarse membranes. Chop half the clams, leaving remaining clams whole.

3. Sauté salt pork in a heavy kettle until pork is golden. Add onions and leeks and sauté until tender.

4. Measure liquid saved from clams and add water to make up to 2 quarts. Add to kettle with chopped tomatoes, canned tomatoes, celery, parsley, thyme, bay leaf, potatoes, salt and pepper. Bring to a boil and simmer covered about 30 to 40 minutes.

5. Blend flour with butter and add a little at a time to hot soup while stirring. Add biscuits, Worcestershire, Tabasco and reserved clams. Reheat and test for seasoning.

Puree of
Oyster Soup

Yield: 6 to 8 servings

6 tablespoons butter
½ cup finely chopped onion
2 packages (10 ounces each)
    frozen green peas
2 cups milk
1 quart shucked fresh
    oysters with their liquor

2 cups clam juice
½ cup dry white wine
Salt and black pepper
    to taste
2 cups heavy cream

1. Melt 2 tablespoons butter in a saucepan and cook onions until they are wilted but not brown. Add peas and milk and simmer just until peas are tender.

2. Add oysters and clam juice and simmer over very low heat 5 minutes or until oysters curl.

3. Add wine, remaining butter, salt and pepper. When butter melts, puree half the mixture in an electric blender.

4. Pour into a saucepan. Then puree remaining mixture and add to saucepan.

5. When ready to serve, preheat broiler and whip cream seasoned with a little salt.

6. Heat soup almost to boiling and spoon it into hot, heatproof serving dishes. Top each serving with a generous spoonful of whipped cream and slide under broiler until cream is toasted dark brown. Serve immediately.

Fish Soup

Yield: 6 to 8 servings

3 tablespoons olive oil
1 cup chopped leeks
3 cloves garlic, finely
    minced
1 cup chopped onion
1¾ cups chopped tomatoes
½ teaspoon thyme
2 sprigs parsley
1 bay leaf
1 cup dry white wine
2 cups water
1 teaspoon leaf saffron,
    crumbled
Salt and black pepper
    to taste
¼ teaspoon Tabasco sauce

1 lobster (1½ pounds)
3 tablespoons butter
1½ teaspoons flour
1 pound fresh red snapper,
    striped bass, porgy or
    other white fish, cut
    into serving pieces
1 quart fresh mussels,
    scrubbed well
2 dozen cherrystone clams
12 shrimp, shelled
    and deveined
1 tablespoon Pernod or
    other anise-flavored
    liqueur
Garlic croutons

1. Heat olive oil in a large saucepan and add leeks, garlic and onion. Cook until wilted; add tomatoes, thyme, parsley, bay leaf, wine, water, saffron, salt, pepper and Tabasco. Simmer 10 minutes.

2. Plunge a knife into center point where tail and carcass meet on lobster. Split tail and carcass. Cut carcass in half lengthwise. Scoop out liver and coral and place in a small mixing bowl. Cut tail section into 4 pieces crosswise.

3. Add carcass and any scraps of lobster to tomato mixture. Cover and simmer 30 minutes.

4. Meanwhile, blend butter and flour with fingers, then mix with reserved coral and liver.

5. Strain tomato mixture through sieve, pushing through as many solids as possible. Bring to a boil and add snapper, mussels, clams, shrimp and reserved lobster tail. Simmer 15 minutes. Stir in coral mixture; when mixture boils, add Pernod. Scoop into hot soup plates and serve with garlic croutons on top.

Tuna Soup with Capers

Yield: 6 or more servings

3 pounds fish bones

2½ cups water

3 sprigs parsley

1 small rib celery with leaves

3 tablespoons butter

¾ cup minced green pepper

1 cup finely minced onion

1 cup finely minced celery

2 cloves garlic, finely minced

¼ cup flour

1 pound cubed boneless fish such as flounder, cod or red snapper

Salt and black pepper to taste

½ teaspoon thyme

Cayenne pepper

2 cans (7 ounces each) water-packed tuna

⅓ cup drained capers

1. Combine fish bones, water, parsley and celery in a saucepan. Simmer 15 minutes. Drain and reserve the stock.

72

2. In a 1½-quart saucepan, heat butter and add green pepper, onion, minced celery and garlic. Cook, stirring occasionally, until vegetables are wilted. Sprinkle with flour.

3. Add fish and fish stock, stirring. Add salt, pepper, thyme and cayenne and simmer until fish flakes easily. Beat the soup briskly to break up the fish.

4. Flake and mash tuna and add it to the soup. Add capers. Bring to a boil and simmer 5 minutes.

Cucumber and Yogurt Soup

Yield: 4 servings

1 medium-size cucumber,
    peeled and diced
Salt
2 cups plain yogurt
2 cups chilled chicken
    broth
1 tablespoon olive oil

2 tablespoons finely
    chopped walnuts
1½ cloves garlic, finely
    minced
Black pepper
1 tablespoon chopped
    chives

1. Sprinkle cucumber with salt; let stand 20 to 30 minutes.

2. Beat yogurt and add broth and olive oil slowly to give a smooth mixture. Rinse cucumber pieces to remove excess salt. Drain well.

3. Add cucumber, walnuts and garlic to yogurt and season to taste with pepper. Chill. Serve soup, garnished with chives, in cold bowls.

Cold Cream of Turnip Soup

Yield: 8 servings

6 to 8 white turnips
4 tablespoons butter
3½ cups chicken broth
2 cups cubed raw
    potatoes

3 cups heavy cream
Salt and black pepper
Tabasco sauce
½ teaspoon Worcester-
    shire sauce

1. Peel turnips and cut them into 1-inch cubes.

2. Melt butter in a large saucepan and add turnips. Cook, stirring occasionally, about 15 minutes. Do not brown. Add chicken broth and potatoes and simmer until vegetables are tender but not mushy, about 20 minutes. Put the mixture through a sieve or food mill. Chill thoroughly.

3. When ready to serve, stir in cream and season with salt and pepper. Add dash of Tabasco and the Worcestershire.

Vichyssoise Piquante

Yield: About 10 servings

3 leeks	4 cups chicken broth
1 cup chopped onion	¼ teaspoon Tabasco sauce
3 tablespoons butter	1 cup heavy cream
3 cups cubed raw	Salt and black pepper
potatoes	Cubed tomato
½ teaspoon leaf saffron	Chopped scallions or chives

1. Trim off end stems of leeks. Cut off and discard green part. Split leeks lengthwise down center and rinse leaves well under cold running water. Chop leeks coarsely. Drain well.

2. Cook leeks and onion in butter; stir until onion is wilted. Add potatoes; stir and cook about 3 minutes. Sprinkle with saffron and add chicken broth. Bring to a boil and skim the surface as necessary. Cook 20 minutes or until potatoes are thoroughly tender. Put soup through a food mill and chill.

3. Add Tabasco and cream to soup. Season to taste with salt and pepper. Serve in chilled cups and garnish with bits of cubed tomato and chopped scallions or chives.

Blueberry Soup

Yield: 4 servings

1 pint fresh blueberries	¼ teaspoon nutmeg
2 cups water	1 lemon, thinly sliced
½ cup sugar	2 cups sour cream
1 three-inch cinnamon stick	½ cup dry red wine

1. Wash and drain blueberries. Combine them with water, sugar, cinnamon, nutmeg and lemon. Bring to a boil and simmer, uncovered, about 15 minutes.

2. Strain the mixture and discard pulp. Chill the liquid. Just before serving, when soup is very cold, beat in sour cream and wine.

Cold Cherry Soup with Farina

Yield: 4 servings

2 cans (1 pound each) pitted sour cherries

1½ tablespoons cornstarch

⅓ cup sugar

½ cup dry red wine

1¾ cups water

1 two-inch cinnamon stick

⅓ cup farina

2 cups milk

2 egg yolks

¼ to ½ cup sugar (see note)

1. Place cherries and liquid in a saucepan. Mix cornstarch and sugar together and gradually stir in wine. Add to cherries.

2. Add water and cinnamon stick; bring to a boil and simmer 5 minutes. Cool and chill.

3. Mix remaining ingredients in a saucepan and bring to a boil, stirring constantly. Simmer 2 minutes. Pour into a shallow dish; cool and chill.

4. Just before serving, remove cinnamon stick and spoon farina mixture into soup. Serve as appetizer, soup, main course or dessert.

Note: The amount of sugar depends on which course of meal soup will be.

Cantaloupe Soup

Yield: 6 servings

1 large ripe cantaloupe 2 tablespoons lime juice
½ teaspoon cinnamon Fresh mint sprigs
2¼ cups orange juice

1. Remove seeds from melon and cube the pulp. Place pulp and cinnamon in an electric blender and puree.

2. Combine orange and lime juices and stir in puree. Chill. Serve in chilled bowls; garnish with mint sprigs.

Hungarian Apple Soup

Yield: 4 to 6 servings

1 pound firm, ripe apples

2 cloves

¼ teaspoon cinnamon

Juice of ½ lemon

⅓ cup sugar

½ cup dry white wine

2 cups milk

½ cup heavy cream

2 tablespoons flour

1. Peel and core apples and place in a saucepan. Add water to cover, cloves, cinnamon, lemon juice and sugar. Simmer until tender. Put through a sieve or food mill. Return to a boil.

2. Add wine and milk, stirring constantly. Remove from heat.

3. Blend the cream and flour and stir into soup. Return the soup to a boil and simmer 5 minutes. Chill.

Fish and Shellfish

Rice-Stuffed Bass

Yield: 6 servings

¼ cup chopped onion

4 tablespoons butter

¼ cup dry bread crumbs

2 cups cooked rice

1½ teaspoons salt

½ teaspoon black pepper

½ teaspoon basil

1 teaspoon snipped fresh
   dill

1 tablespoon chopped
   parsley

2 tablespoons lemon juice

1 fresh bass (3 to 4 pounds)
   Paprika

1. Preheat oven to 400 degrees.

2. Sauté onion in 2 tablespoons butter until tender but not browned. Mix with bread crumbs, rice, ½ teaspoon salt, ¼ teaspoon pepper, basil, dill, parsley and 1 tablespoon lemon juice. Mix well.

3. Clean and dress the fish, cutting almost through on the underside. Fill the cavity thus formed with the rice stuffing. Fasten with skewers and thread.

4. Extra stuffing may be placed alongside the fish in a buttered baking dish. Season fish with remaining salt and pepper.

5. Combine remaining butter and lemon juice and brush over fish. Sprinkle with paprika. Bake 10 minutes a pound or until fish flakes easily, basting frequently with the lemon butter.

Note: A 3- to 4-pound whitefish may be substituted for the bass.

Poached Striped Bass

Yield: 8 servings

1 fresh striped bass (6 to 7 pounds), cleaned but with head left on

Water to cover

1 cup dry white wine

2 carrots, sliced

1 onion, sliced

2 slices lemon

2 sprigs fresh thyme or ½ teaspoon dried

1 bay leaf

1 clove

4 sprigs parsley

Salt to taste

15 peppercorns

1. Rinse fish under cold running water and dry well.

2. Combine remaining ingredients in an oval fish cooker and bring to a boil. Simmer 15 minutes and let cool.

3. Add fish and cover. Simmer 25 minutes or until fish flakes easily. Serve with hollandaise sauce (page 251).

Crab-Stuffed Bluefish

Yield: 4 servings

1 fresh bluefish (3 pounds), cleaned and split	Salt and black pepper
	⅛ teaspoon thyme
4 ounces lump crab meat	1 tablespoon lemon juice
2 tablespoons bread crumbs	4 tablespoons melted butter

1. Preheat oven to 425 degrees.

2. Place bluefish flat in an oiled shallow baking dish.

3. Remove cartilage from crab meat and toss lightly with bread crumbs, salt, pepper, thyme, juice and 1 tablespoon melted butter.

4. Spread stuffing over half of fish; fold over other half and secure with toothpicks or tie.

5. Season fish with salt and pepper and pour remaining butter over it. Bake until fish flakes easily, 20 to 25 minutes.

Fresh Cod Maître d'Hôtel

Yield: 6 servings

1 fresh codfish (6 pounds), boned and skinned

1 clove garlic, thinly sliced

3 sprigs thyme or ½ teaspoon dried

1 onion, sliced

15 peppercorns

½ bay leaf

2 sprigs parsley

Salt to taste

6 medium-size potatoes

5 tablespoons butter

4 tablespoons flour

1 cup heavy cream

1 tablespoon finely chopped parsley

¼ teaspoon cayenne pepper

1 tablespoon finely chopped chives

Coarse salt (Maldon or kosher salt)

Black pepper

1. It is best to have the fish boned and skinned by the fish man. Be certain, however, to remove all small bones he may have overlooked.

2. Place filleted fish in one layer in a skillet. Add garlic, thyme, onion, peppercorns, bay leaf, parsley sprigs, salt and water to cover. Bring to a boil and simmer 10 minutes. Turn off heat and let fish stand in broth until ready to serve.

3. Meanwhile, place potatoes in a large saucepan and add salted water to cover. Cook until tender.

4. Melt 3 tablespoons butter and stir in flour, using a wire whisk. Carefully pour off and strain 2 cups of broth and add it, stirring, to the butter-flour mixture. When mixture is thickened and smooth, simmer 20 minutes, stirring occasionally. Add cream and simmer 20 minutes longer, stirring occasionally. Add chopped parsley, cayenne and chives. Remove from heat; swirl in remaining butter.

5. Carefully transfer fish from the broth to a warm serving platter. Peel potatoes and slice them around fish. Pour hot sauce over all and serve immediately with coarse salt and black pepper on the side.

Barbecued Halibut Steaks

Yield: 4 servings

2 tablespoons chopped
  onion
2 tablespoons chopped
  green pepper
2 tablespoons salad oil
¼ cup soy sauce
½ cup dry white wine
½ cup chopped skinned
  tomatoes
1 clove garlic, finely
  chopped

2 tablespoons lemon juice
2 tablespoons finely
  chopped fresh ginger
  or 1 teaspoon powdered
2 pounds thick, boned
  halibut steaks (see note)
½ pound mushrooms,
  sliced
3 tablespoons butter

1. Sauté onion and green pepper in oil. Add remaining ingredients except fish, mushrooms and butter. Bring to a boil and simmer 1 minute. Cool.

2. Pour over the fish, arranged in a shallow dish. Marinate in refrigerator 30 minutes to 2 hours, turning twice.

3. Remove fish and place in a hinged wire broiler. Reserve marinade. Grill over hot coals, turning once, until fish flakes easily, 10 to 15 minutes.

4. Meanwhile, sauté mushrooms in butter. Add marinade and heat. Pour over cooked fish.

Note: If desired, use any other firm-fleshed white fish, cut into serving pieces.

Florida Keys
Red Snapper

Yield: 4 to 6 servings

1 fresh red snapper
(3 to 4 pounds)
Peanut or vegetable oil
Salt and black pepper
¼ cup butter
½ cup finely chopped onion
¼ cup finely chopped
celery
¼ cup finely chopped
green pepper
2 scallions, chopped

2 cups toasted bread
crumbs
¼ cup finely chopped
parsley
¼ cup coarsely chopped
toasted almonds
6 thin slices tomato
6 thin slices onion
6 thin slices orange
6 thin slices lime
Juice of ½ lime

1. Preheat oven to 350 degrees.

2. Rub snapper lightly with oil and sprinkle inside and out with salt and pepper.

3. Melt butter and cook onion, celery, green pepper and scallions until onion is wilted. Stir in bread crumbs, parsley and almonds. Season to taste with salt and pepper. Stuff fish with mixture and tie with string.

4. Place fish on a length of aluminum foil and add slightly overlapping slices of tomato, onion, orange and lime. Sprinkle with salt, pepper and lime juice. Bring up the edges of the foil and secure it, envelope fashion.

5. Bake 30 minutes, or until fish flakes easily when tested with a fork.

Salmon Mousse

Yield: 6 to 8 servings

2 to 2½ pounds fresh
    poached salmon (see note)
1 cup homemade
    mayonnaise (page 244)
½ cup heavy cream
1 envelope unflavored
    gelatin
¾ teaspoon salt
¼ teaspoon black pepper
3 tablespoons chopped
    parsley
2 tablespoons chopped
    scallions

1 tablespoon chopped
    chives
1 tablespoon chopped
    fresh tarragon
2 tablespoons lemon
    juice, or to taste
2 teaspoons Dijon mustard
Salad greens
Ripe olives or truffles
Scallions and capers

1. Bone, skin and flake fish roughly. Strain the cooking broth and reserve ½ cup.

2. Place ¼ of the fish, ¼ of the mayonnaise and ¼ of the cream in an electric blender and blend until smooth, pushing mixture down with a rubber spatula when necessary. Turn into a bowl and repeat the blending with the remaining ¾ fish, mayonnaise and cream in 3 stages. Alternately, the salmon may be forced through a sieve and mixed with mayonnaise and cream.

3. Soak gelatin in reserved fish broth or salmon liquid.

4. Add salt, pepper, parsley, chopped scallions, chives, tarragon, lemon juice and mustard to fish. Stir to mix.

5. Dissolve gelatin over low heat and stir into salmon mixture. Pour into a lightly oiled 6-cup mold and chill well. Unmold onto a bed of greens and garnish with olives or truffles, scallions and capers.

Note: Canned salmon may be substituted for the fresh. Use 2 cans (1 pound each); drain salmon and reserve ½ cup liquid.

Creamed Salmon with Sherry

Yield: 4 servings

2 cups cooked salmon or	1½ cups milk
1 can (1 pound)	2 egg yolks
salmon, drained	½ teaspoon Worcestershire
½ cup sliced mushrooms	1 teaspoon salt
6 tablespoons butter	1 teaspoon lemon juice
1½ tablespoons flour	3 tablespoons dry sherry

1. Flake the salmon and discard any bones and skin.

2. Cook mushrooms in 2 tablespoons butter until wilted and lightly browned. Heat remaining butter in a saucepan and stir in flour. Stir in milk and cook over medium heat, stirring constantly, until thickened. Remove sauce from heat and add yolks, whisking rapidly.

3. Add remaining ingredients, the salmon and mushrooms and cook about 2 minutes over very low heat, stirring constantly. Serve over rice or toast triangles.

Sole and Asparagus

Yield: 4 servings

1 pound asparagus spears

4 sole fillets (about 1 pound)

Salt to taste

⅛ teaspoon black pepper

½ teaspoon grated lemon
rind

3 tablespoons melted
butter

2 tablespoons lemon juice

1 tablespoon finely
chopped shallot

1 teaspoon Dijon mustard

1. Preheat oven to 400 degrees.

2. Cut asparagus into 2- to 3-inch lengths. Cook in lightly salted boiling water 5 minutes; drain.

3. Season the skin side of fillets with salt, pepper and lemon rind. Place asparagus spears at one end of each fillet. Roll up fillets, with spears inside, and secure with toothpicks. Place in a well-buttered baking dish.

4. Combine remaining ingredients; pour over fish. Bake until fish flakes easily, 15 to 20 minutes, basting twice.

Sole Florentine Casserole

Yield: 6 servings

3 tablespoons butter

3 tablespoons flour

3 cups milk

1 tablespoon lemon juice

1 teaspoon dry mustard

1 teaspoon Worcestershire sauce

½ teaspoon salt

⅛ teaspoon black pepper

⅛ teaspoon nutmeg

1½ cups shredded sharp Cheddar cheese

8 ounces medium egg noodles, cooked al dente and drained

2 packages (10 ounces each) frozen chopped spinach, cooked and very well drained

1½ pounds sole fillets (about 6 medium-size pieces)

¼ cup toasted slivered almonds

1. Preheat oven to 375 degrees.

2. Melt butter in a pan; stir in flour. Slowly stir in milk. Cook, stirring constantly, until sauce thickens and boils 1 minute.

3. Stir in lemon juice, mustard, Worcestershire, salt, pepper, nutmeg and 1 cup cheese. Stir until cheese is melted.

4. Mix together cooked noodles and half the cheese sauce. Pour into a 2-quart baking dish. Top with spinach.

5. Arrange fish fillets on spinach; pour remaining sauce over fish. Sprinkle with remaining cheese and nuts. Bake until fish is cooked, about 20 minutes.

Swordfish Shish

Yield: 4 servings

1 clove garlic, smashed	3 drops Tabasco sauce
¼ cup chopped parsley	1½ pounds swordfish, cubed
¼ cup lemon juice	12 cubes sweet onions
⅔ cup peanut or salad oil	12 cubes green pepper
Salt and black pepper to taste	12 cherry tomatoes
½ teaspoon thyme	½ cup butter

1. Combine garlic, parsley, lemon juice, oil, salt, pepper, thyme and Tabasco. Stir to blend and add the swordfish. Refrigerate an hour or so, turning the fish occasionally.

2. Alternate cubes of swordfish, onion and green pepper and the cherry tomatoes on skewers. Grill, turning once, until fish flakes easily, 5 to 10 minutes. Push onto a plate a unit at a time or the tomatoes will shatter. Pour hot, melted butter seasoned with juice of ½ lemon over all.

Swordfish à l'Espagnole

Yield: 3 or 4 servings

1 swordfish steak (1 pound)
Salt and black pepper
6 tablespoons olive oil
1 onion, finely chopped
1 clove garlic, minced
¼ cup chopped parsley
½ teaspoon thyme

1 large tomato, skinned
and chopped
1 bay leaf
2 tablespoons tomato paste
½ cup dry sherry
½ cup water
3 slices lemon

1. Preheat oven to 350 degrees.
2. Sprinkle fish with salt and pepper. Pour 2 tablespoons olive oil into a shallow baking dish. Add fish.
3. Cook onion, garlic, parsley and thyme in remaining oil until wilted. Add tomato, bay leaf and salt to taste. Cook until well mixed. Add tomato paste, sherry and water and simmer 5 minutes longer. Pour this over fish. Add lemon slices and bake 30 minutes, basting occasionally.

Trout Meunière

Yield: 6 servings

6 fresh trout	Vegetable oil
1 cup (approximately) milk	4 tablespoons butter
⅓ cup (approximately) flour	Lemon wedges
1 teaspoon salt	Parsley sprigs
¼ teaspoon black pepper	

1. Clean fish and rinse inside and out under cold running water. Leave heads on, if desired.

2. Arrange trout in a pan; add enough cold milk to cover fish. Let stand 30 minutes or longer.

3. Drain fish but do not dry them. Coat fish, one at a time, in flour seasoned with salt and pepper. If necessary, use more flour.

4. Add just enough oil to a large skillet to cover the bottom ¼ inch deep.

5. Cook trout until they are golden brown on one side. Carefully turn each and cook until golden brown on the other side. Transfer trout to a warm serving platter and keep warm.

6. Quickly pour off oil from the skillet and wipe skillet with absorbent toweling. Add butter and cook until nut brown. Do not burn. Immediately pour butter over the fish and serve with lemon wedges. Garnish with parsley.

Sea Food Mold

Yield: 12 appetizer portions or 6 main-dish servings

¼ cup cold milk

1 envelope unflavored
  gelatin

2 tablespoons butter

1 teaspoon curry powder

1 small apple, peeled
  and diced

1 small onion, diced

½ cup chicken broth

½ teaspoon Worcestershire
  sauce

2 tablespoons lemon juice

¼ teaspoon Tabasco sauce

½ cup mayonnaise

1 cup sour cream

2 tablespoons chutney

½ pound (1½ cups) lump
  crab meat, cooked
  shrimp or lobster, or a
  combination

1. Put cold milk and gelatin in an electric blender; cover and blend at low speed to soften gelatin.

2. Melt butter in a skillet. Add curry powder, apple and onion. Cook until apple and onion are tender but not browned.

3. Add broth to skillet; bring to a boil and add to milk-gelatin mixture in blender. Blend briefly to dissolve gelatin.

4. Turn control to high speed and add remaining ingredients except sea food. Blend until smooth. Stop blender and fold in picked-over or diced sea food. Turn into a lightly oiled 3½-cup mold and chill until firm, 4 hours or overnight. Unmold.

New England Clam Pie

Yield: 6 to 8 servings

2 quarts soft-shell long neck clams	1 teaspoon sugar
2 cups cubed raw potatoes	3 tablespoons butter
1 onion, finely chopped	3 tablespoons flour
Salt and black pepper to taste	1 cup milk
	Pie pastry made from 1½ cups flour

1. Wash clams in several changes of lukewarm water.

2. Drain clams and place in a kettle. Add 2 cups cold water and bring slowly to a boil. When clams open, remove from heat. Strain clam broth through a double thickness of cheesecloth; reserve broth.

3. Remove clams from shells. Dip each clam into broth; snip off and discard dark heads. Strain the broth again and chop clams.

4. Preheat oven to 400 degrees.

5. Place potato cubes and onion in a saucepan and add 1 cup salted water. Bring to a boil; cover and simmer until potatoes are tender. Add pepper, sugar, chopped clams and clam broth. Bring to a boil.

6. Blend butter and flour with fingers. Stir, bit by bit, into simmering stew. Bring milk to a boil and add to stew. Remove from heat.

7. Butter a 1½-quart pie dish or casserole generously and pour in the clam mixture. Cover with rolled-out pie pastry and prick with a fork or make small slashes with a knife.

8. Bake 30 minutes or until pastry is golden. Serve hot.

Stuffed Mussels

Yield: 4 servings

2 dozen raw mussels

½ cup chopped parsley

2 tablespoons fresh basil

1 tablespoon fresh oregano

½ cup freshly grated
    Parmesan cheese

2 cloves garlic, minced

Salt and black pepper
    to taste

1 cup fresh bread crumbs

¼ cup olive oil

1. Preheat oven to 500 degrees.

2. Scrub mussels very well to remove all sand and the beards. Using sharp, thin knife, open mussel shells, running knife horizontally so that mussels are halved. Discard half the shell, but leave mussel in the other. Cut around mussel.

3. Combine parsley, basil, oregano, cheese, garlic, salt and pepper in a mixing bowl.

4. Add bread crumbs to herb mixture. Toss until well mixed. Stir in olive oil.

5. Spoon or sprinkle equal parts of the mixture onto mussels. Arrange in a baking dish and bake until crumb mixture is golden brown, 5 minutes or longer. Serve hot.

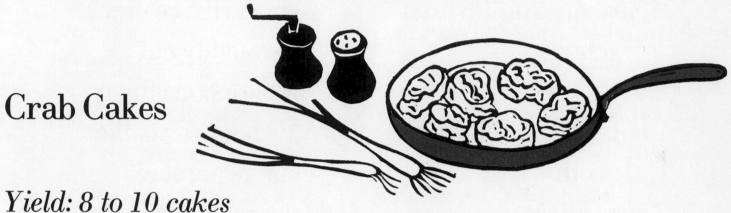

Crab Cakes

Yield: 8 to 10 cakes

¼ cup chopped parsley
3 tablespoons chopped
   scallions, including
   green part
1 pound crab meat, picked
   over

½ teaspoon salt
⅛ teaspoon black pepper
1 teaspoon dry mustard
1 egg, lightly beaten
½ cup fine bread crumbs
½ cup butter

Combine parsley, scallions, crab meat, salt, pepper, mustard and egg and mix well. Shape into small cakes. Roll in bread crumbs and cook in butter until golden brown on all sides.

Crab Meat Mousse

Yield: 6 servings

2 envelopes unflavored
    gelatin
2 tablespoons dry sherry
1 cup boiling chicken
    broth
2 egg yolks
1 cup heavy cream
3 tablespoons lemon juice
5 drops Tabasco sauce
1½ to 2 cups crab meat,
    picked over and
    flaked

2 small ribs celery,
    roughly cut
2 tablespoons finely
    chopped scallion
4 sprigs parsley
¼ teaspoon marjoram
¼ teaspoon thyme
½ cup homemade
    mayonnaise (page 244)
Field lettuce

1. Place gelatin and sherry in an electric blender and set aside for 2 minutes. Add chicken broth and blend at low speed 10 seconds or until gelatin is dissolved.

108

2. While continuing to blend at low speed, add egg yolks, cream, lemon juice, Tabasco, crab meat, celery, scallion, parsley, marjoram and thyme. Blend until smooth and well mixed.

3. If the size of the container allows, add mayonnaise and blend 10 seconds. If not, pour mixture into mayonnaise and use a wire whisk to mix. Pour into a lightly oiled 6-cup mold. Chill.

4. Unmold onto platter and garnish with field lettuce.

Sautéed Scallops Provençale

Yield: 4 to 6 servings

6 tablespoons olive oil

2 cloves garlic, finely chopped

1 shallot, finely chopped

1½ pounds bay or sea scallops, quartered if large, rinsed, drained and dried

1 teaspoon lemon juice

1 large ripe tomato, skinned, chopped and seeded

Salt and black pepper to taste

¼ cup finely chopped parsley

1. Heat oil in a heavy skillet and sauté garlic and shallot until tender but not browned. Increase heat and add scallops. Sauté until scallops are lightly browned and opaque, about 5 minutes.

2. Add lemon juice, tomato, salt, pepper and parsley. Cook just long enough to heat through.

Broiled Scallops with Lemon

Yield: 6 to 8 servings

2 pounds scallops
   Salt and black pepper
   to taste
6 leaves fresh basil,
   chopped, or 1 teaspoon
   dried

2 sprigs fresh rosemary or
   ½ teaspoon dried
1 lemon, thinly sliced
   Tabasco sauce to taste
¼ cup salad oil

1. If bay scallops are used, leave them whole. If large sea scallops are used, cut them in half. Place in bowl with remaining ingredients. Cover and refrigerate 2 hours or longer.

2. Remove scallops from marinade and arrange in one layer in a shallow baking dish. Broil about 3 minutes, then turn and broil 3 minutes longer, until barely cooked through. Do not overcook scallops or they will toughen.

111

Scallop Quiche

Yield: 6 servings

1½ cups bay scallops or
    sliced sea scallops
    (about 1 pound)
2 tablespoons minced
    celery with leaves
2 tablespoons finely
    chopped parsley
¼ cup dry white wine
½ teaspoon salt

¼ teaspoon black pepper
1 unbaked 9-inch
    pie shell, chilled
5 eggs, lightly beaten
1½ cups heavy cream,
    scalded
2 tablespoons freshly
    grated Parmesan
    cheese

1. Preheat oven to 450 degrees.

2. Combine scallops, celery, parsley, wine, salt and pepper and spoon into pie shell.

3. Combine eggs and cream and pour over scallop mixture. Sprinkle with cheese and bake 10 minutes. Reduce heat to 350 degrees and bake 20 minutes longer or until set.

Curried Shrimp Creole

Yield: 6 servings

6 strips bacon
2 cups finely chopped onion
2 cups minced celery
1 cup minced green pepper
1 clove garlic, minced
½ cup minced parsley
1 bay leaf
2 sprigs fresh thyme or
   1 teaspoon dried

6 cups canned Italian
   plum tomatoes
Salt and black pepper
   to taste
2 teaspoons curry powder
Cayenne pepper to taste
2 pounds shrimp, shelled
   and deveined

1. Cut bacon into small cubes and cook in an iron or heavy saucepan until rendered of fat. Add onion, celery, green pepper and garlic; cook, stirring, until onion is translucent.

2. Add remaining ingredients except shrimp. Bring to a boil and simmer 30 minutes, stirring occasionally.

3. Add shrimp to sauce and cook 10 to 15 minutes longer.

113

Shrimp and Cucumber

Yield: 4 servings

1 pound large shrimp, shelled and deveined	1 tablespoon dry sherry
2 medium-size cucumbers	1 teaspoon sugar
3 tablespoons vegetable oil	¼ teaspoon monosodium glutamate
1 tablespoon chopped scallion	2 teaspoons cornstarch
2 teaspoons salt	1 tablespoon toasted sesame seeds

1. Cut the shrimp in half lengthwise; cut each half into bite-size pieces. Peel cucumbers, quarter lengthwise and remove seeds. Cut into bite-size pieces.

2. Heat 1 tablespoon oil in a heavy skillet and sauté scallion and cucumber until transparent, about 3 minutes. Remove from the skillet and sprinkle with 1 teaspoon salt; reserve.

3. Heat remaining oil in the skillet.

4. Mix shrimp with sherry, remaining salt, sugar, monosodium glutamate and cornstarch. Sauté until pink.

5. Return cucumbers to pan and cook, stirring, 2 minutes longer. Stir in sesame seeds.

Scampi

Yield: 4 servings

¼ cup butter	¼ teaspoon black pepper
2 pounds large shrimp, shelled and deveined	2 cloves garlic, chopped
	¼ cup chopped parsley
½ teaspoon salt	Lemon wedges

1. Heat butter in a skillet and fry shrimp about 5 minutes, or until cooked, shaking pan over high heat. Sprinkle shrimp with salt and pepper and place on a hot serving plate.

2. Add garlic and parsley to butter remaining in skillet. Stir for 30 seconds and pour over shrimp. Serve scampi with lemon wedges.

Crab-Stuffed Shrimp

Yield: 4 servings

20 large shrimp (2 pounds)
¼ pound mushrooms,
    finely chopped
8 tablespoons butter
1 pound fresh crab meat
1 hard-cooked egg,
    chopped
3 scallions, finely chopped
2 tablespoons minced
    parsley

½ cup dry sherry
½ teaspoon oregano
Salt and black pepper
    to taste
1 cup fresh bread crumbs
1½ cups heavy cream
½ cup freshly grated
    Parmesan cheese

1. Preheat oven to 350 degrees.

2. Peel and devein shrimp. Slit them down the back so they will open "butterfly" style.

3. Cook mushrooms in a skillet in 2 tablespoons butter, stirring constantly, until liquid evaporates.

116

4. Place picked-over crab meat in a mixing bowl; flake it. Add mushrooms, egg, scallions, parsley, sherry, oregano, salt, pepper, crumbs and enough cream to bind mixture.

5. Fill the open part of each shrimp with a heaping portion of the crab mixture. Arrange shrimp, stuffed side up, in a baking dish. Sprinkle with cheese and remaining butter, melted. Bake 15 minutes.

Shrimp-Stuffed Eggplant

Yield: 4 to 6 servings

2 medium eggplants
6 tablespoons butter or
    bacon fat
1 onion, finely chopped
1 clove garlic, finely minced
1 green pepper, seeded
    and finely chopped
2 ribs celery, finely chopped
½ cup finely chopped parsley
1 teaspoon chopped fresh
    thyme or ½ teaspoon
    dried
1 tablespoon chopped fresh
    basil

1 cup cooked shrimp,
    coarsely chopped
Salt and black pepper
    to taste
1 teaspoon Worcestershire
    sauce
Tabasco sauce to taste
2 eggs
1 cup dry toast crumbs
¼ cup freshly grated
    Parmesan cheese

1. Preheat oven to 350 degrees.

2. Split eggplants in half and scoop out the flesh, leaving a shell about ¼ inch thick. Drop eggplant flesh into boiling salted water and cook until tender. Drain it in a colander.

3. Cover eggplant shells with boiling water and let stand 5 minutes. Drain.

4. Melt half the butter and cook onion, garlic, green pepper and celery until onion is translucent. Add eggplant flesh, parsley, thyme, basil, shrimp, salt, pepper, Worcestershire and Tabasco.

5. Add eggs to eggplant mixture. Cook, stirring, about 5 minutes. Fill the eggplant shells with mixture.

6. Sprinkle crumbs over filled eggplants. Melt remaining butter and pour over the eggplants.

7. Bake 20 to 30 minutes. Sprinkle with Parmesan cheese. Serve hot.

Shrimp Rémoulade

Yield: 4 to 6 servings

2 pounds shrimp
1 bay leaf
1 rib celery with leaves
2 sprigs parsley
12 peppercorns
   Salt to taste
3 tablespoons tarragon
   vinegar
3 tablespoons Dijon
   mustard
5 anchovies, finely chopped
¾ cup oil (this may be a
   mixture of olive oil and
   salad oil)

Black pepper
½ teaspoon chopped fresh
   tarragon or ¼ teaspoon
   dried
1 clove garlic, finely minced
1 tablespoon chopped
   parsley
1 scallion, including
   green part, chopped
3 tablespoons horseradish
Tabasco sauce to taste

1. Peel and devein shrimp. Reserve shrimp shells.

2. Place shrimp, shells, bay leaf, celery, parsley, peppercorns and salt in a saucepan and add water to cover. Bring to a boil and simmer about 5 minutes. Drain and cool.

3. Place shrimp in a mixing bowl. Chill. Combine remaining ingredients and pour over shrimp. Let stand overnight in refrigerator. Bring to room temperature before serving on bed of chopped lettuce.

Paella à la Giner

Yield: 10 servings

¾ cup Spanish olive oil

1 frying chicken (3 pounds),
   cut into 2-inch pieces

1 pound lean pork, cubed

1 teaspoon paprika

1 onion, finely chopped

3 cloves garlic

½ teaspoon whole saffron

1 quart chicken broth,
   warmed

2 cups long-grain rice

2 teaspoons salt

2 tablespoons finely
   chopped parsley

1 cup lima beans (see note)

1 pound unshelled shrimp,
   washed

1 large tomato, cut into
   wedges

1 green pepper, cubed

1 quart clams, scrubbed

1. Pour oil into paella pan set over a fire of twigs or low heat; make sure pan is level. Add chicken and pork pieces and cook slowly until well browned, 20 to 25 minutes, stirring occasionally with a wooden spoon.

2. Sprinkle meat with paprika and stir. Add onion and cook 5 minutes longer.

3. Crush garlic with a mortar and pestle until well mashed. Add saffron and crush. Stir in 1 tablespoon broth. Add to cooked meat in pan along with rice. Stir to coat rice with oil.

4. Slowly add remaining broth, salt, parsley and lima beans. Bring to a boil. Simmer slowly, stirring occasionally, until rice is barely tender, about 15 minutes.

5. Add remaining ingredients and cook until rice and shrimp are cooked and clams open, 8 to 10 minutes. If mixture appears to be getting too dry at any point during the cooking, extra chicken broth may be added.

Note: If frozen lima beans are used, they will need less cooking time and may be added with shrimp.

Shrimp Duglère

Yield: 4 to 6 servings

2 pounds shrimp, shelled
  and deveined
¼ cup flour
  Salt and black pepper
8 tablespoons butter
2 tablespoons finely
  chopped shallots
½ cup dry white wine

1½ cups heavy cream
2 tablespoons each finely
  chopped parsley and
  fresh tarragon
18 skinned cherry tomatoes
  (see note)
2 tablespoons lemon juice

1. Dredge shrimp in flour seasoned with salt and pepper. Heat 6 tablespoons butter in a large skillet; cook shrimp until lightly browned on one side. Turn and brown lightly on the other. Transfer to a warm platter.

2. Add shallots and 1 tablespoon butter to skillet. Add wine and cook, stirring around bottom and sides, until wine is almost totally evaporated.

3. Add cream, parsley and tarragon and bring to a boil. Add shrimp and cherry tomatoes; heat. Season to taste with salt and pepper. Swirl in remaining butter and lemon juice. Serve with rice.

Note: Cover cherry tomatoes with boiling water; leave 15 to 30 seconds; pour off water and peel tomatoes.

Shrimp and Salmon Aspic

Yield: 4 to 6 servings

2 cups strained homemade
　　chicken broth
6 peppercorns
6 whole allspice
1 bay leaf
6 sprigs fresh dill
2 envelopes unflavored
　　gelatin
½ cup cold water
1½ cups fish stock (made by
　　concentrating liquid
　　used to cook fish)

1 cup cooked, shelled,
　　deveined shrimp
2 hard-cooked eggs (one
　　sliced and one
　　quartered)
2 cups cooked salmon,
　　mackerel or eel,
　　skinned, boned and
　　flaked
1 cup diced celery
Boston lettuce
Mayonnaise

1. Place chicken broth in a saucepan. Add peppercorns, allspice, bay leaf and dill tied in a muslin bag. Bring to a boil and simmer 10 minutes. Remove bag.

2. Soften gelatin in cold water. Add to hot broth and stir to dissolve. Add fish stock and cool until mixture starts to jell.

3. Arrange shrimp in a 6-cup mold or loaf pan and spoon half the gelatin mixture over it. Chill until almost firm.

4. Arrange eggs in a pattern around the edge of the mold and spoon half the remaining gelatin over them. Chill.

5. Add flaked fish and celery and spoon over last of gelatin. Chill several hours or overnight. Unmold onto lettuce and serve with mayonnaise.

Shrimp Mornay

Yield: 4 to 6 servings

2 tablespoons butter

2 tablespoons flour

1 cup milk (use ½ cup fish stock if available)

½ cup grated Gruyère or sharp Cheddar cheese

¼ cup heavy cream

Salt and black pepper to taste

1 pound shrimp, cooked, shelled and deveined

2 tablespoons freshly grated Parmesan cheese

1. Melt butter and blend in flour. Gradually stir in the milk. Bring to a boil, stirring.

2. Stir in Gruyère until it melts.

3. Add cream and season to taste with salt and pepper.

4. Divide shrimp among 4 to 6 greased ramekins or serving shells. Pour sauce over shrimp and sprinkle with Parmesan. Place under broiler, 4 inches from source of heat, and cook until bubbly hot and lightly browned.

Poultry and Game

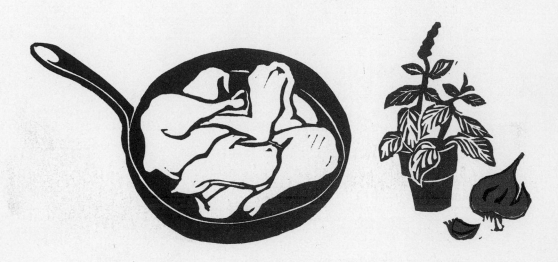

Chicken Pie

Yield: 6 servings

1 fowl (4 to 5 pounds)
1 carrot, quartered
2 ribs celery with leaves
2 sprigs parsley
½ small onion, sliced
6 peppercorns
Salt
8 tablespoons butter
4 tablespoons flour
¼ cup heavy cream
2 tablespoons dry sherry
1 pound mushrooms, sliced if large
2 tablespoons diced pimentos
2 tablespoons diced green pepper
Pastry or biscuit topping

1. Place fowl, carrot, celery, parsley, onion, peppercorns, 1 teaspoon salt and just enough water to cover the bird in a deep casserole or pot. Cover and simmer about 1 hour or until tender. Allow bird to cool slightly in broth.

2. Skin and bone chicken. Cut meat into large chunks. Boil broth used to cook the fowl until it is concentrated in flavor. Strain and measure 2 cups and reserve.

3. Preheat oven to 400 degrees.

4. Melt 3 tablespoons butter; blend in flour and gradually stir in reserved chicken broth. Bring to a boil and cook, stirring, until sauce thickens.

5. Season to taste with salt and pepper and add cream, sherry and mushrooms sautéed in remaining butter. Stir in chicken, pimentos and green pepper.

6. Place creamed chicken mixture in a shallow baking dish. Top with pastry or biscuit dough; make hole for escape of steam and bake about 25 minutes or until done. Or, if desired, creamed chicken mixture may be reheated and served on rice or toast points as chicken à la king.

Chicken Barbecue

Yield: 4 servings

2 chickens (2½ to 3 pounds each), split for broiling

¾ cup butter, melted

¼ cup vegetable oil

¼ cup dry white wine

½ teaspoon Worcestershire sauce

½ teaspoon Tabasco sauce

Juice of 1 lemon

Salt and black pepper

1. If a grill is used, place chickens skin side down on the grill. Or place them skin side up under preheated broiler.

2. Add remaining ingredients to butter and brush over chicken. Grill or broil without turning until chickens are golden to dark brown on cooked side. Brush occasionally as they cook. When the skin side is brown, turn and brush with sauce. Continue cooking over moderate heat while basting until chickens are done. The total cooking time should be 45 minutes to an hour.

Chicken with Lime

Yield: 6 servings

2 chickens (2½ to 3 pounds each), cut into serving pieces
8 limes or lemons
1 cup cornmeal

1 cup flour
Salt and black pepper
2 pounds lard or 1 quart vegetable shortening
½ pound butter

1. Place chicken pieces in a mixing bowl. Squeeze limes and pour juice over chickens. Cover and refrigerate an hour or so, turning the chicken pieces occasionally in the juice.

2. Sift together cornmeal, flour, salt and pepper.

3. Heat half the lard and half the butter in each of 2 skillets.

4. Coat the chicken, one piece at a time, in cornmeal mixture. Add chicken pieces to the hot fat. Cook until golden brown on one side, turn and cook until golden brown on the other. As pieces are cooked, drain on absorbent toweling.

133

Chicken Sauté
au Parmesan

Yield: 4 servings

1 chicken (2½ to 3 pounds), cut into serving pieces

Salt and black pepper

4½ tablespoons butter

1½ tablespoons flour

¾ cup milk

¼ cup heavy cream

¼ teaspoon nutmeg

½ cup freshly grated Swiss or Gruyère cheese

½ cup freshly grated Parmesan cheese

2 tablespoons fresh bread crumbs

1. Sprinkle chicken with salt and pepper and brown on all sides in 3 tablespoons butter. This should require about 20 minutes.

2. Preheat oven to 350 degrees.

3. Melt remaining butter in a saucepan; stir in flour. When blended, add milk and cream, stirring rapidly.

134

4. When mixture is boiling, thickened and smooth, remove from heat and stir in nutmeg and Swiss cheese.

5. Sprinkle a baking dish with half the Parmesan cheese and arrange chicken pieces over it. Spoon sauce over chicken and sprinkle with remaining Parmesan and bread crumbs.

6. Bake until golden brown and chicken is cooked, about 20 minutes.

Chicken and Vegetable Curry

Yield: 8 servings

2 chickens (2½ to 3 pounds each), cut into serving pieces
2½ teaspoons salt
¾ teaspoon turmeric
½ cup shortening
2 large onions, sliced
2 ribs celery, diced
2 carrots, sliced
1 green pepper, diced

2 teaspoons curry powder
¼ teaspoon cinnamon
¼ teaspoon cloves
½ teaspoon ginger
1 tablespoon flour
1 bay leaf
2 cups chicken broth
2 tomatoes, skinned and chopped

1. Rub chicken pieces with 1 teaspoon salt and ¼ teaspoon turmeric.

2. In a large heavy skillet, brown chicken pieces in shortening, turning to brown evenly. Remove chicken; reserve.

136

3. Add onions, celery, carrots and green pepper to the fat remaining in skillet. Sauté until onions are barely tender. Sprinkle with curry powder and remaining turmeric and cook 2 minutes.

4. Sprinkle vegetables with cinnamon, cloves, ginger and flour and cook, stirring, a few seconds. Add remaining ingredients, including remaining salt, and bring to a boil, stirring.

5. Return chicken to skillet and cook, covered, over low heat until chicken is tender, about 30 minutes.

Chicken Paprika

Yield: 8 servings

¼ cup butter

8 medium-size onions, sliced

2 tablespoons sweet
   Hungarian paprika

2 chickens (3 pounds each),
   cut into serving pieces

Salt and black pepper

1 cup chicken broth

3 tablespoons flour

½ cup light cream

½ cup sour cream

1. Heat butter in a heavy skillet; add onions and cook until golden but not browned. Add paprika and mix.

2. Season chicken with salt and pepper. Add chicken pieces to skillet; cook over medium heat 15 minutes, turning once.

3. Add chicken broth; cover and cook 20 minutes or until chicken is tender.

4. Mix flour with light cream. Add a little of the hot broth, return to the pan and cook, stirring until thickened.

5. Stir in sour cream and reheat but do not boil.

Chicken with Basil

Yield: 4 servings

1 chicken (3 to 4 pounds), cut into serving pieces	½ cup dry white wine
Salt and black pepper	¾ cup chopped tomatoes
2 tablespoons butter	½ cup chicken broth
¼ cup chopped shallots	4 leaves fresh basil
½ clove garlic, minced	1 bay leaf
	2 sprigs parsley

1. Sprinkle chicken pieces with salt and pepper. Brown chicken in butter. Remove and reserve.

2. Add shallots and garlic to skillet and cook briefly over low heat, stirring. Add wine; stir to dissolve brown particles clinging to skillet. Cook until wine is almost evaporated.

3. Add tomatoes, chicken broth, basil, bay leaf and parsley; simmer about 5 minutes. Season; return chicken to sauce. Cover and cook until chicken is tender, about 25 minutes. Remove bay leaf and parsley and serve with fluffy rice.

Spicy Chicken

Yield: 4 servings

1 chicken (2½ to 3
   pounds), cut into
   serving pieces
⅓ cup flour
   Salt and black pepper
2 tablespoons oil
1 onion, chopped
1 clove garlic, finely
   chopped
4 tomatoes, skinned and
   quartered
1½ cups dry white wine

½ teaspoon thyme
½ teaspoon oregano
½ teaspoon crushed hot red
   pepper, or to taste
2 carrots, diced
1 cup pimento-stuffed
   olives
12 dried prunes
1 large plantain or 3 green
   bananas, peeled and
   sliced
1 tablespoon sugar

1. Rub chicken pieces with flour seasoned with the salt and
   black pepper.

2. Heat oil in a heavy skillet and brown chicken pieces on all sides. Add onion and garlic and sauté until onion is tender.

3. Add tomatoes, wine, thyme, oregano, red pepper, carrots and olives. Cover and simmer 15 minutes or until chicken is nearly tender.

4. Add remaining ingredients and salt and pepper to taste. Cover and cook 10 to 15 minutes or until prunes are tender.

Orange Chicken

Yield: 4 servings

1 chicken (2½ to 3 pounds), cut into serving pieces

Salt and black pepper

¼ cup butter

2 tablespoons oil

3 tablespoons orange juice

1½ tablespoons grated orange rind

½ teaspoon rosemary

2 teaspoons chopped parsley

Orange slices

1. Season chicken with salt and pepper. Combine remaining ingredients except orange slices and heat, stirring.

2. Place chicken pieces on a broiler pan or barbecue grill 6 to 8 inches from charcoal fire. Brush with orange-butter mixture and broil slowly, turning frequently and brushing with the mixture, until chicken is golden brown and done, about 45 minutes. Garnish with orange slices.

142

Chicken Pepitoria

Yield: 4 servings

1 chicken (2½ to 3 pounds), cut into serving pieces

¼ cup (approximately) olive oil

1 slice stale bread, broken

1 onion, finely chopped

2 cloves garlic

2 hard-cooked egg yolks

10 toasted blanched almonds, chopped

1 cup chicken broth

¼ cup dry sherry

1 tablespoon chopped parsley

1. Preheat oven to 350 degrees.

2. Brown chicken pieces in oil. Transfer to a casserole. In remaining oil, fry bread until golden; drain. Sauté onion and garlic, adding oil if necessary, until golden.

3. Remove garlic and mash with yolks and almonds to form a paste. Thin paste with broth and sherry; add to onion. Simmer 5 minutes. Pour over chicken. Sprinkle with parsley and bread. Bake, uncovered, about 35 minutes.

143

Chicken Dijonnaise

Yield: 4 servings

1 chicken (3 pounds), cut into serving pieces
Salt and black pepper
3 tablespoons butter
1 tablespoon finely chopped shallot
½ cup dry white wine
1 cup chicken broth

½ teaspoon tarragon
½ teaspoon thyme
½ bay leaf
2 egg yolks
½ cup sour cream
1 tablespoon Dijon or Düsseldorf mustard

1. Sprinkle chicken with salt and pepper. Melt 2 tablespoons butter in a skillet and brown chicken on all sides.

2. Remove chicken to a warm place and add remaining butter to skillet. Add shallots and cook, stirring, without browning. Add wine and cook, stirring around the bottom and sides, until all brown particles are dissolved. Simmer until almost all wine evaporates.

3. Add chicken broth, tarragon, thyme and bay leaf. Return chicken to skillet; cover and simmer until chicken is tender, about 30 minutes.

4. Remove chicken to serving platter and strain sauce into saucepan. Beat yolks lightly and add to sauce. Cook, stirring constantly, until sauce thickens. Do not overheat or yolks might curdle. Stir in sour cream and mustard. Reheat but do not boil. Pour over chicken. Serve immediately.

Chicken in Cream with Tarragon

Yield: 4 servings

1 chicken (3 pounds), cut into serving pieces

Salt and black pepper to taste

5 tablespoons butter

1 teaspoon chopped fresh tarragon or ½ teaspoon dried

2 teaspoons finely chopped shallots

½ cup dry white wine

1 cup heavy cream

4 tablespoons flour

1 tablespoon warm apple-jack or cognac

1. Sprinkle chicken with salt and pepper.

2. Heat 2 tablespoons butter and brown chicken on all sides. Sprinkle with tarragon. Cover and cook about 15 minutes. Sprinkle with shallots and wine. Cover again and simmer 10 minutes longer or until chicken is cooked.

146

3. Remove chicken to a warm dish and keep warm. Add the heavy cream to the skillet gradually, stirring constantly with a whisk. Bring to simmering point.

4. Blend remaining butter and flour with the fingers and add to the sauce, stirring with the whisk. Add just enough of butter-flour mixture to give desired consistency.

5. Add chicken and season to taste with salt and pepper. Stir applejack into sauce. When applejack is added, the dish may be flamed if desired.

Mrs. Abbas Ordoobadi's Fesenjan

(Chicken in Pomegranate Sauce)

Yield: 10 servings

5 whole chicken breasts

1 rib celery

½ teaspoon thyme

2 sprigs parsley

1 bay leaf

5 tablespoons butter

2 large onions, chopped

3 tablespoons tomato sauce

3 cups finely ground walnuts

2½ cups water

3 tablespoons lemon juice

1 teaspoon salt

1 teaspoon cinnamon

¾ cup pomegranate juice
(see note)

⅓ cup sugar

1. Place chicken breasts in a large skillet and barely cover with water. Sprinkle center of celery rib with thyme; tie it in cheesecloth with parsley and bay leaf and add to skillet. Simmer chicken until tender, about 10 minutes. Cool.

2. Bone chicken, discarding skin, and divide each breast into 6 to 8 pieces.

3. Heat butter in a saucepan and sauté onions until golden. Add tomato sauce and cook 5 minutes. Add walnuts and cook very slowly 5 minutes longer, stirring continuously to avoid sticking. Add remaining ingredients and simmer, covered, 40 minutes. Add more sugar or salt if needed.

4. Add chicken to sauce and cook slowly 20 minutes. Serve with *shirin polo* (orange-almond rice); see page 262.

Note: Pomegranate juice is available at M. Kehayan, 380 Third Avenue (at 28th Street), New York City.

Chicken Gismonda

Yield: 4 servings

2 large whole chicken
    breasts, split in half,
    skinned and boned
Flour for dredging
Salt and black pepper
2 eggs, lightly beaten
1 tablespoon water
¼ cup freshly grated
    Parmesan cheese

½ cup fresh bread crumbs
¾ cup butter
1½ pounds spinach
½ pound mushrooms,
    thinly sliced
1 tablespoon lemon juice
¼ teaspoon nutmeg

1. Coat chicken breasts lightly but thoroughly in flour seasoned with salt and pepper.

2. Beat eggs with water and dip chicken in the mixture. Blend cheese and bread crumbs; coat pieces thoroughly in this mixture. Pat lightly to help crumbs adhere.

150

3. Melt ½ cup butter in a large skillet and cook chicken in it until golden brown on both sides, turning once.

4. Meanwhile, rinse spinach well and place it in a saucepan with a tight-fitting lid. Do not add additional water or salt. Cover and cook briefly, stirring once or twice, until spinach is crisp but tender.

5. While spinach cooks, heat half the remaining butter in a skillet and cook the mushrooms in it, stirring, until light brown.

6. Drain spinach well and toss with remaining butter and lemon juice. Season with salt and nutmeg.

7. Spoon hot spinach onto 4 hot plates and top with chicken breasts. Scatter mushrooms over all and serve hot.

Mrs. William G. Mennen's Chicken Livermore

Yield: 4 to 6 servings

3 whole chicken breasts,
   split in half, skinned
   and boned
   Salt and black pepper
¼ cup butter
1 clove garlic, finely
   chopped
2 tablespoons finely
   chopped shallots
¼ pound mushrooms, sliced

2 tablespoons flour
½ cup dry white wine
½ cup chicken broth
1 bay leaf
¼ teaspoon thyme
⅛ teaspoon marjoram
2 tablespoons chopped
   parsley
½ cup heavy cream

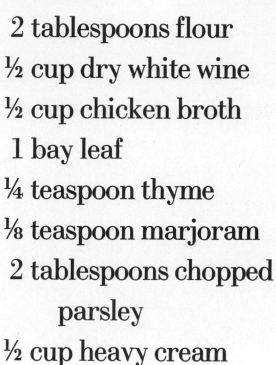

1. Season chicken breasts with salt and pepper. Melt butter
   in a heavy skillet and brown chicken on all sides quickly.
   Remove breasts to a warm platter.

152

2. Add garlic, shallots and mushrooms to butter in skillet; cook 3 minutes. Sprinkle with flour and cook 2 minutes, stirring. Blend in wine and broth slowly.

3. Add herbs and bring to a boil, stirring to scrape all the cooked-on particles into the sauce. Simmer 5 minutes.

4. Return chicken to pan and cook until tender, about 8 minutes. Do not overcook.

5. Transfer breasts to a warm dish. Add cream to liquid in pan and simmer 3 or 4 minutes. Season to taste with salt and pepper and pour over chicken.

Note: This dish can be prepared ahead up to end of Step 4, then refrigerated until 10 minutes before serving. It should be reheated very slowly so as not to overcook the chicken, and then finished.

Chicken with Eggplant

Yield: 6 servings

2 medium-size eggplants

½ pound skinned boneless
   breast of chicken

1 tablespoon cornstarch

2 tablespoons soy sauce

1 tablespoon dry sherry

2 fresh hot green peppers
   or dried red pepper
   flakes to taste

¼ cup peanut oil

1 small clove garlic,
   finely minced

1 tablespoon freshly grated
   ginger or ½ teaspoon
   powdered

½ cup chicken broth

1. Peel eggplants and slice into ¼-inch rounds. Slice each round into very thin, matchlike strips. There should be about 4 cups of strips. Pour boiling water over eggplant and let stand 5 minutes. Drain well in a colander.

2. Cut chicken into thin slices; then cut each slice into thin, matchlike strips. Place chicken strips in a mixing bowl.

3. Add cornstarch, soy sauce and sherry to chicken strips.

4. Split peppers in half and discard the seeds and stem end. Cut peppers into thin strips. Increase or decrease the amount of peppers according to taste.

5. Heat oil and cook peppers until they start to color. Remove peppers with a spoon. Add chicken and cook, stirring briskly, until flesh turns white. Add eggplant strips, garlic, peppers, ginger and chicken broth. Cook just until mixture boils, is slightly thickened and eggplant is tender. Serve hot.

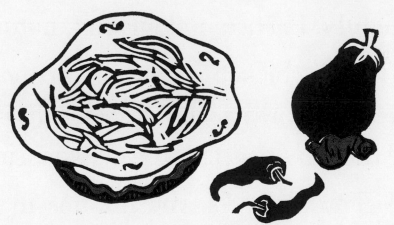

Chicken Breasts au Porto

Yield: 4 servings

2 whole chicken breasts,
   split in half, skinned
   and boned
½ cup flour
1 teaspoon salt
¼ teaspoon nutmeg

¼ teaspoon black pepper
6 tablespoons butter
1½ cups heavy cream
¼ cup port wine
½ pound mushrooms, sliced

1. Place chicken breasts between wax paper and pound lightly. Dredge in flour, salt, nutmeg and pepper.

2. Brown chicken in 4 tablespoons butter. Remove and reserve. Add 1 cup cream, stirring. Simmer 2 minutes. Add wine and chicken. Cover; simmer about 5 minutes.

3. Meanwhile, cook mushrooms in remaining butter until wilted. Add remaining cream and bring to a boil. Pour over chicken; season to taste. Cover; simmer 8 to 10 minutes longer or until chicken is tender. Do not overcook.

Chicken Croquettes

Yield: 9 croquettes

¼ cup butter

⅓ cup flour

1 teaspoon salt

1 cup milk

2 cups finely diced
    cooked chicken

1 tablespoon grated onion

1 tablespoon lemon juice

1 tablespoon chopped
    parsley or fresh
    tarragon

1 egg, lightly beaten

⅓ cup fresh bread crumbs

⅓ cup vegetable oil

1. Melt butter and blend in flour and salt. Stir in milk gradually and cook, stirring, until mixture thickens. Cook over low heat 3 minutes; cool.

2. Stir in chicken, onion, lemon juice and chopped parsley. Spread mixture in an 8-inch square pan. Chill.

3. Shape mixture into 9 cutlets; dip first in beaten egg and then in bread crumbs. Fry in hot oil until brown.

Chicken with Green Pepper Strips

Yield: 6 servings

2 cups sliced mushrooms	2 teaspoons curry powder
5 tablespoons butter	2 teaspoons flour
4 cups cooked chicken, in bite-size pieces	1 onion, sliced into rings
2 cups chicken broth	2 green peppers, cut into strips
Salt and black pepper	1 cup toasted whole almonds

1. Cook mushrooms in 3 tablespoons butter until wilted. Add chicken, broth, salt, pepper and curry powder.

2. Blend remaining butter with flour. When well kneaded stir, bit by bit, into simmering chicken mixture. Cook about 10 minutes over low heat, stirring occasionally.

3. Add onion rings and green peppers and cook about 3 minutes. The green peppers should retain much of their crisp texture. Serve sprinkled with toasted almonds.

Curried Turkey

Yield: 4 servings

1 tart apple, chopped
1 large onion, chopped
1 clove garlic, chopped
6 tablespoons butter
1 large green pepper, chopped
3 ribs celery, chopped

1 tablespoon flour
2 tablespoons curry powder
2 tablespoons lime juice
1½ cups chicken broth
1 teaspoon ginger
2 cups diced cooked turkey
½ cup heavy cream

1. Sauté apple, onion and garlic in butter until tender. Add green pepper and celery. Cook 1 minute longer.

2. Sprinkle with flour and curry powder and stir while cooking 2 minutes. Add juice, broth and ginger and bring sauce to a boil, stirring until it thickens. Cover and simmer 10 minutes.

3. Add turkey and heat 5 minutes. Stir in cream and reheat. Serve with traditional side dishes.

Stuffed Turkey Breast

Yield: 8 to 12 servings

1 boned turkey breast
(10 pounds)
Salt and black pepper
4 strips bacon, diced
½ pound butter
1 onion, chopped
1 clove garlic, minced

½ teaspoon thyme
½ teaspoon rosemary
1 bay leaf, chopped
2 hard-cooked eggs, chopped
2 sprigs parsley, chopped
2 cups fresh bread crumbs

1. Preheat oven to 350 degrees.

2. Place turkey skin side down on a board and open it up to receive stuffing. Season with salt and pepper.

3. Cook bacon and half the butter over low heat until bacon is cooked but not brown. Add onion, garlic, thyme, rosemary and bay leaf. Cook, stirring, about 10 minutes. Cool slightly and add remaining ingredients.

4. Spoon stuffing into the center of breast and bring sides of breast together to enclose stuffing. Sew opening with string. When ready, turkey will look vaguely heart shaped.

5. Place turkey, sewn side down, in a roasting pan and dot with remaining butter. Sprinkle with salt and pepper and roast, basting, 2½ hours or until tender. If gravy is desired, add 1 cup water to the drippings in the pan and stir until all brown particles are dissolved. Simmer briefly and strain. Serve hot.

Cornish Hens Ménagère

Yield: 6 to 12 servings

6 Rock Cornish hens	1 clove garlic, split
Salt and black pepper	½ cup butter
½ cup chopped parsley	2 small onions, sliced
6 large cubes (about 2-inch squares) of day-old French or Italian bread with crusts	½ teaspoon thyme
	¾ cup cold water

1. Preheat oven to 425 degrees.

2. Sprinkle inside of each hen with salt and pepper.

3. Cut hen livers in half and sprinkle with salt and pepper. Toss with parsley.

4. Rub bread cubes on all sides with garlic clove. Stuff each hen cavity with equal portions of the liver mixture and a cube of bread. Truss hens.

162

5. Melt butter in a heatproof shallow baking dish and turn the hens to coat on all sides. Add gizzards, necks, onions and thyme. Lay hens on one side and roast, basting, 10 minutes. Turn and continue roasting and basting 10 minutes. Lay hens on backs and roast, basting, 10 minutes longer.

6. Remove the trussing from hens and spoon some of the cooking fat into the interiors. Add the water to the pan and return hens to the oven for 5 minutes. Serve split in half.

Cornish Hens Hawaiienne

Yield: 6 servings

6 Rock Cornish hens	2 slices preserved ginger,
½ cup butter	chopped
1 teaspoon salt	Juice of ½ lemon
¼ teaspoon black pepper	1 tablespoon cornstarch
2 cloves garlic, minced	3 tablespoons cold water
1 cup chicken broth	2 tablespoons chopped
¼ cup ginger syrup	parsley

1. Sauté hens in butter in a large skillet or Dutch oven, turning until golden. Sprinkle with salt, pepper and garlic. Cook about 5 minutes. Add broth, cover and cook until tender, about 30 minutes. Remove hens; keep warm.

2. To the juices in skillet, add ginger syrup, chopped ginger and lemon juice. Bring to a boil. Stir in cornstarch mixed with cold water and cook, stirring, until sauce is thickened. Add parsley, return hens to sauce and cook 5 minutes.

Duck Mountain Style

Yield: 4 servings

¼ cup olive oil

1 tablespoon paprika

1 duck (4 to 5 pounds), quartered

1 medium-size onion, chopped

¼ cup flour

2 cups chicken broth

½ cup dry sherry

1 medium-size tomato, skinned and sliced

¼ cup chopped pimento-stuffed green olives

1. Combine olive oil and paprika in a heavy skillet; mix well. Add duck; cook until browned on all sides and remove.

2. Add onion to drippings and cook 5 minutes. Add flour and mix well. Gradually add broth and sherry and cook over low heat, stirring constantly, until thickened.

3. Add tomato, olives and duck. Cover and cook over low heat 1 hour or until duck is tender.

Mrs. Joseph Amico's
Roast Duck with Sour Cherries

Yield: 4 servings

1 duck (5 to 6 pounds)	1 medium-size carrot, sliced
½ teaspoon salt	1 can (No. 2) sour pitted
⅛ teaspoon black pepper	cherries
Pinch of thyme	½ cup port wine
2 small onions, sliced	1 teaspoon cornstarch

1. Preheat oven to 425 degrees.

2. Season inside of duck with salt, pepper, thyme and half the onion slices. Prick skin around thighs, back and lower breast.

3. Place duck, breast side up, in a roasting pan and add remaining sliced onion and carrot around it. Roast 15 minutes to brown lightly. Reduce heat to 350 degrees and turn duck on its side.

4. After 30 minutes, turn duck on other side. Thirty minutes later, turn breast side up and salt lightly. Cook 15 to 30 minutes longer, depending on desired degree of doneness. Each time duck is turned, the fat in the pan should be drained off.

5. Remove duck to a warm platter. Remove all but 1 tablespoon fat from pan; add juice drained from cherries and wine. Bring to a boil, stirring well. Strain into small saucepan; add cornstarch dissolved in a little cold water and heat until thickened. Add cherries; heat through. Serve with duck.

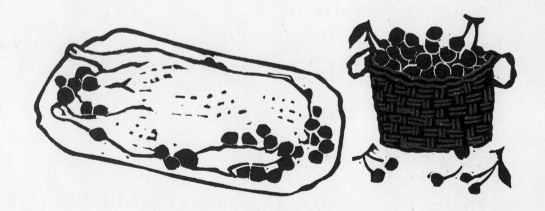

Squab with Madeira Sauce

Yield: 2 servings

4 strips fat bacon, halved

2 tablespoons finely
   chopped shallots or
   scallions

½ clove garlic

½ teaspoon salt

¼ teaspoon black pepper

5 tablespoons butter

¼ teaspoon thyme

2 squabs (10 to 12 ounces
   each), cleaned

2 three-inch rounds of
   bread

¾ cup brown gravy or
   brown sauce

2 tablespoons Madeira

Watercress sprigs

1. Preheat oven to 400 degrees.

2. Simmer bacon strips in water 8 minutes. Drain and dry on paper towels.

3. Make a paste of 1 tablespoon shallots, the garlic, salt, pepper, 1 tablespoon butter and the thyme. Spoon into cavities of birds and truss. Tie bacon pieces over breasts and thighs.

4. Place squabs on their sides on a rack in a roasting pan; roast about 40 minutes or until tender and no pink juice comes from leg joint. Turn once during cooking and baste frequently with 2 tablespoons butter, melted.

5. Melt 1 tablespoon of the remaining butter. Brush bread rounds on both sides with the butter and broil, sauté or bake until golden.

6. Melt remaining tablespoon of butter in a small skillet and sauté remaining tablespoon of shallots. Stir in brown gravy; bring to simmering point and add Madeira and meat drippings from the roasting pan.

7. Place each squab atop a crouton and garnish with watercress. Serve sauce separately.

Rabbit with Wine

Yield: 4 servings

¼ pound salt pork, cubed
1 rabbit (3½ pounds), cut
 into pieces
1 teaspoon salt
¼ teaspoon black pepper
2 onions, chopped
1 clove garlic, minced
¼ cup flour
1½ cups chicken broth

½ cup white wine
1 cup canned tomatoes
2 sprigs parsley
1 rib celery, chopped
1 bay leaf
12 small white onions
2 tablespoons chopped
 parsley

1. Cook salt pork in water to cover about 5 minutes. Drain. Brown in a skillet. Remove and reserve.

2. Sprinkle rabbit pieces with salt and pepper and cook a few pieces at a time in the drippings until well browned on all sides. Lower heat to medium; add chopped onions and garlic and cook until vegetables are lightly browned.

3. Stir in flour and cook until flour is lightly browned. Gradually stir in chicken broth and wine and bring to a boil. Add pork cubes, tomatoes, parsley sprigs, celery and bay leaf. Cover and cook over low heat 30 minutes.

4. Add onions; cover and cook 45 minutes longer or until rabbit is tender. Sprinkle with chopped parsley and serve with noodles.

Venison Stew

Yield: 6 servings

½ pound salt pork, diced

3 pounds venison shoulder
   or brisket, cut into
   cubes (see note)

1 rib celery, chopped

3 onions, chopped

1 carrot, sliced

3 tablespoons flour

Salt and black pepper
   to taste

3 cups broth made from
   bones and meat scraps

1 bay leaf

Juice of ½ lemon

2 cloves

½ cup dry red wine

1. Sauté salt pork in a large heavy skillet until lightly browned. Add venison and brown quickly on all sides. Add celery, onions and carrots; cook until wilted.

2. Sprinkle with flour and cook, stirring, 2 minutes. Add remaining ingredients except wine and bring to a boil. Cover and simmer gently about 1 hour or until meat is tender. Stir in wine and cook 15 minutes longer.

Meats

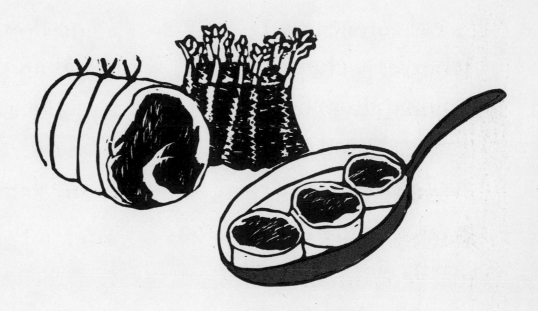

Beef with Caraway
and Sour Cream

Yield: 6 or more servings

1 rump roast of beef
  (3 pounds)
½ cup tomato paste
2 cups beef broth
1 cup dry white wine
¼ cup Madeira, port or
  sherry
1½ cups thinly sliced onion
1 rib celery, coarsely
  chopped

½ teaspoon thyme
½ bay leaf
¼ cup flour
Salt and black pepper
1 to 2 teaspoons caraway
  seeds
¾ cup sour cream

1. Place roast in a large mixing bowl. Combine tomato paste, beef broth, white wine, Madeira, onion, celery, thyme and bay leaf. Spoon mixture over meat, cover and refrigerate 12 hours.

174

2. Preheat oven to 450 degrees.

3. Drain meat and reserve marinade. Dry meat lightly with paper towels and dredge in flour seasoned with salt and pepper. Place meat on a rack and roast, turning until browned on all sides.

4. Transfer meat to a Dutch oven. Add marinade and caraway seeds. Cover; bring to boil on top of stove.

5. Place in oven and reduce heat to 325 degrees. Continue cooking until the meat is fork tender, 2 to 3 hours. When ready, strain sauce; stir in sour cream. Heat thoroughly but do not boil.

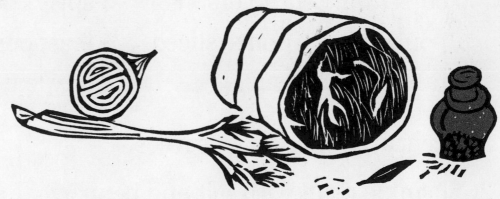

Carbonnade of Beef Flamande

Yield: 6 to 8 servings

3 pounds round steak or chuck, cut into 1-inch cubes	2 cups light beer
	1 cup beef broth
Salt and black pepper	1 tablespoon wine vinegar
¼ pound salt pork, finely diced	1 teaspoon brown sugar
	1 clove garlic, finely minced
5 tablespoons butter	1 leek, trimmed and washed
6 cups thinly sliced onions	3 sprigs parsley
½ pound mushrooms, sliced	½ teaspoon thyme
3 tablespoons flour	1 bay leaf

1. Preheat oven to 325 degrees.

2. Sprinkle meat with salt and pepper.

3. Place salt pork in a small saucepan and cover with water. Simmer 1 minute and drain well.

4. Heat 1 tablespoon butter in a large skillet and add salt pork. Cook over moderate heat until browned. Remove pork with a slotted spoon and drain on paper toweling.

5. Brown a few cubes of beef at a time in the remaining fat. As meat is browned, transfer it to a heavy casserole with lid.

6. Heat remaining butter in skillet and cook onions, stirring frequently, just until brown. Add mushrooms and cook 3 or 4 minutes. Add flour to the skillet and cook, stirring, over very low heat until flour starts to brown.

7. Gradually add beer and broth, stirring and scraping vigorously with a wire whisk. When mixture is thickened and smooth, add vinegar, sugar and garlic and return to a boil. Add sauce and salt pork cubes to the meat in casserole.

8. Tie leek, parsley, thyme and bay leaf in a muslin bag and add it to casserole. Sprinkle with salt and pepper; cover. Bake 1½ to 2 hours, or until meat is fork tender. Serve with buttered noodles or steamed potatoes.

Beef Ragout

Yield: 6 servings

3 pounds lean beef, round or chuck, cubed

2 teaspoons salt

¼ teaspoon black pepper

2 tablespoons (approximately) salad oil

2 tablespoons butter

1 medium-size onion, chopped

1 carrot, chopped

2 ribs celery, chopped

2 cloves garlic, minced

½ cup flour

2 cups beef broth

2 cups dry red wine

2 fresh tomatoes, skinned and chopped, or 1 cup canned Italian plum tomatoes

4 sprigs parsley

2 bay leaves

¼ teaspoon thyme

12 small white onions

6 carrots, halved

12 small potatoes, peeled

1 tablespoon chopped parsley

1. Sprinkle meat with salt and pepper. Heat oil and butter in a skillet and brown meat on all sides over high heat, adding more oil if necessary.

178

2. Lower heat to medium. Add chopped onion, chopped carrot, celery and garlic; cook until onion is lightly browned.

3. Stir in flour and cook until flour is blended. Gradually stir in beef broth and wine and bring to a boil. Add tomatoes, parsley sprigs, bay leaves and thyme. Cover and cook over low heat 1½ hours.

4. Add the whole onions, halved carrots and potatoes. Cover again and continue cooking 1 hour longer. Sprinkle with parsley before serving.

Hungarian Goulash

Yield: 6 servings

2 pounds beef chuck or veal, cut into large chunks
Salt and black pepper
¼ cup butter
6 to 8 medium-size onions, sliced

2 to 4 tablespoons sweet Hungarian paprika
1 tablespoon flour
Beef or chicken broth
2 cups sour cream

1. Season meat with salt and pepper and brown in butter. Add onions and enough paprika to color meat and onions well. Cook, stirring, about 5 minutes.

2. Sprinkle with flour; stir to mix.

3. Add just enough broth to cover meat. Cover tightly and simmer until meat is tender.

4. Stir in sour cream. Reheat but do not allow to boil.

Chili con Carne

Yield: About 16 servings

⅓ cup olive oil

16 cloves garlic, finely chopped

4 pounds beef chuck, cut into small cubes

½ cup good grade chili powder, or to taste

2 tablespoons ground cumin

4 teaspoons oregano

4 cups (approximately) beef broth

⅓ cup masa harina or fine cornmeal

1. Heat oil in a Dutch oven or heavy kettle. Sauté garlic and meat in batches until well browned.

2. Return all to pan. Sprinkle with chili powder; add cumin, oregano and broth. Bring to a boil; cover and simmer very slowly 6 hours or longer. Add more broth as necessary.

3. Mix the masa harina with a little cold water and stir into chili. Cook, stirring, until thickened.

Mexican Flank Steak

Yield: 8 or more servings

1 flank steak

2 tablespoons bacon fat

1½ cups minced onion

¾ cup chopped celery

½ cup finely chopped
   green pepper

3 cloves garlic

1 teaspoon thyme

Salt and black pepper

Tabasco sauce

4 cups crumbled corn
   bread (page 349)

2 eggs, lightly beaten

2 tablespoons hot green
   chili peppers

2 tablespoons finely
   chopped parsley

3 tablespoons peanut oil

½ cup chopped tomatoes

½ cup chopped carrots

1 bay leaf

1 cup beef broth

Chili powder to taste

1. Preheat oven to 350 degrees.

2. Lay steak on a flat surface. Slice steak lengthwise in half to make 2 very thin steaks.

3. Heat bacon fat and add 1 cup onion, ½ cup celery, green pepper and 1 clove garlic, finely chopped. Cook slowly until vegetables are wilted, about 15 minutes, and add ½ teaspoon thyme, salt and pepper and Tabasco to taste.

4. In a mixing bowl, combine corn bread with eggs, chilies and parsley. Add vegetable mixture and mix well.

5. Spread equal parts of filling on each portion of meat. Roll meat up jelly-roll style and tie both rolls in several places with string. Sprinkle with salt and pepper and brown on all sides in peanut oil.

6. Pour off most of fat and add remaining onion, celery, garlic, thyme, tomatoes, carrots and bay leaf. Add broth.

7. Cover closely and bake about 1 hour or until tender. Transfer meat to a serving platter and remove string. Slice meat.

8. Strain gravy remaining in pan into a saucepan; remove surface fat. Add chili powder, bring to a boil and serve hot with meat.

Tournedos

Yield: 4 servings

4 small eggplant slices	3½ tablespoons butter
4 tablespoons olive oil	2 tablespoons chopped
12 skinned cherry tomatoes	shallots
4 tournedos (small filets	⅓ cup Madeira wine
mignons), each about	1 cup brown sauce or
1½ inches thick	canned beef gravy
Salt and black pepper	⅓ cup water

1. Sauté eggplant slices in 3 tablespoons oil until tender and lightly browned. Set aside.

2. Add remaining oil to skillet and cook tomatoes 2 minutes.

3. Sprinkle beef with salt and pepper.

4. Heat 1½ tablespoons butter in a large skillet and when it is golden brown, cook tournedos on all sides until browned. (About 5 minutes a side for rare.) Transfer steaks to a warm platter.

5. Add shallots to skillet and cook briefly, then pour in wine. Add brown sauce and water. Stir to blend and simmer 5 minutes. Add salt and pepper to taste and remove sauce from the heat. Swirl in remaining butter.

6. Top each tournedo with a sautéed eggplant slice and 3 tomatoes. Pour some of the sauce over meat; serve the rest separately.

Steak au Poivre

Yield: 4 servings

4 club or shell steaks
    (12 ounces each),
    about ¾ inch thick
2 tablespoons peppercorns
4 tablespoons butter
3 tablespoons warm cognac

Salt to taste
3 shallots, finely chopped
¾ cup beef broth
1 cup brown sauce or
    canned beef gravy

1. Dry steaks with paper towels. Crush peppercorns with a mortar and pestle; with the heel of the hand, rub pepper into both sides of steaks. Set aside 30 to 90 minutes.

2. Heat 3 tablespoons butter in a large heavy skillet. Sauté steaks quickly, about 3 minutes on each side for medium rare; slightly longer, lowering the heat, for well done.

3. Pour warm cognac over steaks, stand back and ignite.

4. When the flame subsides, remove steaks. Scrape off excess pepper, season with salt and place on a warm platter.

5. Sauté shallots in fat in skillet until tender. Add broth; cook until almost dry. Add brown sauce, bring to a boil and cook 1 to 2 minutes. Swirl in remaining butter. Serve separately.

Bul Kogi
(Korean Barbecued Steak)

Yield: 6 to 8 servings

5 pounds sirloin steak or
   top sirloin roast
½ cup soy sauce
¼ cup sugar
2 tablespoons sesame oil
   or salad oil

1 clove garlic, finely
   minced
4 scallions, chopped
1 teaspoon monosodium
   glutamate

1. Steak or sirloin must be cut across the grain into thin, large slices. Each slice should be about ⅛ inch thick.

2. Combine remaining ingredients and dip the thin slices into the mixture. Let slices stand 30 minutes. Cook the slices on both sides over hot charcoal.

Celery Steak

Yield: 6 servings

1 pound boneless sirloin
    or round steak
1½ teaspoons salt
¼ teaspoon black pepper
3 tablespoons flour
¼ cup vegetable oil
1 medium-size green
    pepper, cut into
    ½-inch strips

1 cup onion rings
1½ cups sliced celery
1 teaspoon finely chopped
    fresh ginger or ¼ tea-
    spoon ground
1 teaspoon turmeric
1 tablespoon lemon juice
1 cup boiling beef broth

1. Have butcher cut meat into 2-by-½-by-¼-inch strips.

2. Rub meat with salt and pepper mixed with flour. Brown in hot oil. Remove and reserve meat.

3. Sauté green pepper, onion and celery in same pan until tender. Return meat to pan and add the remaining ingredients. Cover and simmer 10 minutes or until tender.

Caraway Short Ribs

Yield: 6 to 8 servings

4 pounds short ribs	1 teaspoon caraway seeds
1½ teaspoons salt	1 bay leaf
¼ teaspoon black pepper	½ cup chopped onion
1 cup beef broth	3 carrots, sliced
1 cup tomato juice	8 ounces green beans,
½ teaspoon oregano	cut into 2-inch lengths

1. Brown ribs on all sides in a heavy casserole or Dutch oven. Cover tightly and cook slowly 1 hour. Discard drippings.

2. Add salt, pepper, broth, juice, oregano, caraway seeds, bay leaf and onion. Cover and cook 1 hour or until the meat is almost tender.

3. Add carrots and beans; cook 20 to 30 minutes, until vegetables are tender. To thicken gravy if desired, mix 1½ tablespoons flour with a little cold water for every cup of liquid. Add to saucepan and cook, stirring.

Boiled Beef

Yield: 6 servings

1 brisket of beef	2 ribs celery with leaves
(3 to 4 pounds)	12 peppercorns, bruised
1 shank bone	slightly
8 leeks	Salt to taste
7 carrots	1 bay leaf
1 onion	1 teaspoon thyme
4 cloves	12 white onions

1. Place meat and shank bone in a deep kettle or Dutch oven. Cover with boiling water.

2. Add 2 of the leeks, halved; 1 carrot, quartered; the onion studded with the cloves; celery; peppercorns; salt; bay leaf and thyme.

3. Bring to a boil, cover and simmer 3 hours or until meat is tender.

4. During the last 20 minutes, add all the remaining vegetables. Cook until barely tender.

Serve with: Prepared mustard (preferably Dijon or Düsseldorf), cornichons (small sour pickles), grated fresh horseradish, homemade tomato sauce (page 247), caper or horseradish sauce (page 257), mustard sauce (page 248) or coarse salt, such as kosher.

Party Hamburgers with Sauce

Yield: 24 burgers

5 pounds ground chuck beef

1½ cups tomato juice

1¼ cups fine bread crumbs

1½ tablespoons salt

¾ teaspoon black pepper

Sauce:

1 tablespoon butter

1 small onion, finely chopped

1 clove garlic, finely chopped

¼ cup chopped celery with leaves

2 tablespoons chopped green pepper

2 cups canned or fresh chopped skinned tomatoes

3 tablespoons tomato paste

½ bay leaf

1 tablespoon molasses

1 teaspoon dry mustard

3 tablespoons vinegar

¼ teaspoon cloves

1 teaspoon salt

1 teaspoon Tabasco sauce

1. Mix beef with juice, bread crumbs, salt and pepper and shape into 24 burgers. Store in refrigerator, keeping burgers separated by layers of wax paper.

2. Melt butter in a skillet and sauté onion and garlic until tender but not browned. Add remaining ingredients and simmer 30 minutes. Sauce may be used to brush hamburgers as they are cooking, as well as to spoon over after they are cooked. The same sauce is good on spareribs and chicken.

Tollgate Farm
Meat Balls and Sauerkraut

Yield: 8 to 10 servings

2 pounds ground chuck
    or round beef
¼ cup finely chopped onion
2 teaspoons chopped fresh
    tarragon
1 clove garlic, finely
    chopped
1 teaspoon salt
½ cup soft bread crumbs
2 eggs, lightly beaten
¼ teaspoon black pepper
½ teaspoon Worcestershire
    sauce

½ cup bacon fat
¼ pound slab bacon, sim-
    mered in water 10 min-
    utes, drained and diced
2 cans (1 pound 13 ounces
    each) sauerkraut,
    squeezed dry
1 bay leaf
1 cup dry white wine
2 cups (approximately)
    chicken broth
1 pint sour cream

1. Combine beef, onion, tarragon, garlic, salt, bread crumbs, eggs, pepper and Worcestershire sauce. Mix lightly with the hands. Form into 18 to 24 balls and brown quickly in bacon fat, which has been heated in a heavy skillet. Set aside. Do not cook through.

2. Combine diced bacon, sauerkraut, bay leaf, wine and broth in a heavy Dutch oven or saucepan. Bring to a boil, cover and simmer until most of liquid has been absorbed, 2 to 3 hours. Season to taste with additional salt and pepper.

3. In a heavy casserole or kettle, place a layer of sauerkraut and a layer of meat balls; repeat until all are used. Cover and simmer 1 hour. Add broth if necessary. Just before serving, stir in the sour cream and reheat.

Meat Balls with Eggplant

Yield: 4 to 6 servings

½ pound ground round
    steak
½ pound ground pork or
    veal
1 egg
½ cup fresh bread crumbs
1 tablespoon minced
    parsley
2 tablespoons chopped
    scallion
Salt and black
    pepper to taste

Flour for dredging
6 tablespoons olive oil
1½ cups minced onion
1 clove garlic, minced
1 small eggplant, peeled
    and cubed
2 cups canned tomatoes
1 tablespoon tomato
    paste
½ teaspoon sugar
1 teaspoon oregano

1. Combine meats in a mixing bowl and add egg, bread crumbs, parsley, scallion, salt and pepper.

196

2. Blend well and shape into 24 meat balls. Dredge meat balls in flour. Brown on all sides in half the oil. Set aside.

3. Heat remaining oil in a large skillet and cook onion and garlic until onion is wilted. Add eggplant cubes and toss lightly; season with salt and pepper. Add the remaining ingredients and bring to a boil.

4. Add meat balls; cover and simmer about 40 minutes.

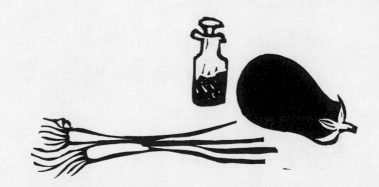

Ham-Stuffed Meat Loaf

Yield: 6 to 8 servings

¾ pound ground chuck
    beef
¾ pound ground lean pork
¾ pound ground veal
¾ cup chicken broth
3 tablespoons prepared
    mustard (preferably
    Dijon)
1⅓ cups soft bread crumbs
1 clove garlic,
    finely chopped
1 onion, chopped

2 tablespoons butter
1 teaspoon salt
1 egg, lightly beaten
¼ teaspoon black pepper
¾ teaspoon thyme
¾ teaspoon basil
1 pound smoked ham,
    ground
½ teaspoon cloves
¼ cup chili sauce
5 hard-cooked eggs

1. Preheat oven to 350 degrees.
2. Combine beef, pork, veal, chicken broth, mustard and bread crumbs in a bowl.

3. Sauté garlic and onion in butter until tender but not browned and add to meat with salt, egg, pepper, thyme and basil. Spread half the mixture in a 9-by-5-by-3-inch loaf pan.

4. Combine ham, cloves and chili sauce; spread a thin layer over meat in loaf pan. Arrange 4 hard-cooked eggs over ham, top or pack around remaining ham.

5. Use remaining beef mixture to fill pan. Set in a shallow pan to catch any drippings and bake 1 hour and 15 minutes. Allow to stand 5 minutes before turning out onto a warm platter. Decorate with remaining egg, sliced.

Flaming Crown Roast of Lamb

Yield: 8 servings

1 crown roast of lamb
    prepared from 2 lamb
    racks (about 16 ribs)
½ cup chopped celery
½ cup chopped onion
½ cup chopped carrots
6 tablespoons melted butter
1 cup bread crumbs
1 teaspoon chopped
    parsley

1 teaspoon chopped
    scallion
½ clove garlic, finely chopped
2 teaspoons flour
2 cups chicken broth
1 bay leaf
2 peppercorns, crushed
    Salt to taste
3 to 4 tablespoons warm
    cognac

1. Preheat oven to 375 degrees.

2. Cover the tips of the rib bones with foil or pieces of potato.

3. Place celery, onion, carrots and 2 tablespoons melted butter in bottom of a roasting pan and place roast on top.

200

4. Mix bread crumbs, remaining butter, parsley, scallion and garlic. Rub all over lamb, coating the outside especially well.

5. Roast about 1 hour or until desired degree of doneness is achieved. Pink lamb will have an internal temperature of 160 to 165 degrees; well-done lamb, 175 to 180 degrees.

6. Remove lamb to an ovenproof platter and keep warm in a low oven. Pour off excess fat from roasting pan. Sprinkle with flour and cook, stirring, 2 minutes.

7. Add broth, bay leaf and peppercorns to roasting pan and bring to a boil, stirring. Simmer 15 to 20 minutes. Strain, season to taste with salt and serve separately. Remove foil or potatoes from rib ends and replace with paper frills, if desired.

8. Garnish platter as desired and place warm cognac in a small chafing dish or pitcher. Pour all over outside of the crown at the table and ignite.

Lemon Lamb Shanks

Yield: 4 to 6 servings

1 clove garlic

4 to 6 lamb shanks

1 teaspoon salt

½ teaspoon black pepper

3 tablespoons flour

1 teaspoon paprika

2 tablespoons shortening

½ cup chicken broth

1 bay leaf

4 peppercorns

2 tablespoons grated lemon
rind

1 cup lemon juice

Lemon wedges

1. Cut garlic into 4 to 6 pieces and insert in gashes made in shanks. Season shanks with salt and pepper. Roll meat in flour mixed with paprika.

2. Brown shanks in shortening in a heavy skillet or Dutch oven. Add remaining ingredients except lemon wedges.

3. Cover and simmer until meat is fork tender, 2 to 2½ hours. Turn occasionally during cooking and add more broth if necessary. Serve garnished with lemon wedges.

Orange-Flavored Lamb Riblets

Yield: 6 servings

½ teaspoon salt

1 teaspoon celery seed

1 teaspoon lemon juice

2 teaspoons prepared mustard (preferably Dijon)

Grated rind from 2 oranges

¼ cup brown sugar

¼ cup vinegar

¼ cup orange juice

1 teaspoon Worcestershire sauce

1 cup canned tomatoes

1 onion, thinly sliced

2 pounds lamb riblets

1. Preheat oven to 350 degrees.

2. Combine all ingredients except lamb in a saucepan; bring to a boil and simmer 10 minutes.

3. Place meat in a dish, casserole or roasting pan. Pour sauce over meat; cover and bake 1 hour or until tender.

4. If desired, riblets may be transferred to a broiler rack and broiled 5 to 8 minutes.

Lamb Chops with Tarragon

Yield: 4 servings

8 loin lamb chops, each about 1½ inches thick

Salt and black pepper

3 tablespoons butter

3 tablespoons finely chopped shallots

⅓ cup dry white wine

1 tablespoon chopped fresh tarragon or 1 teaspoon dried

1⅓ cups brown sauce or canned beef gravy

16 tarragon leaves (optional)

1. Carefully remove bones from lamb chops but leave on a thin layer of fat. Sprinkle with salt and pepper. Roll and secure with toothpicks.

2. Melt 2 tablespoons butter in a heavy skillet; brown chops on all sides, 8 minutes or until desired doneness.

3. Remove chops to a hot platter, arrange neatly and keep warm in a slow oven.

204

4. Pour off fat from skillet and add shallots. Cook, stirring, 1 or 2 minutes. Add wine and cook, stirring, until wine is almost totally evaporated. Add chopped tarragon. Stir in brown sauce and when blended remove from heat. Swirl in remaining butter.

5. Drop tarragon leaves into boiling water and drain immediately. Plunge into cold water. Carefully unfold leaves on paper toweling. Arrange 2 crossed leaves on each chop and serve with sauce.

Navarin d'Agneau
(Spring Lamb Stew)

Yield: 6 servings

3 pounds lean lamb shoulder, cut into serving pieces

3 tablespoons olive oil

1 tablespoon sugar

Salt and black pepper

3 tablespoons flour

2 to 3 cups lamb stock or canned beef bouillon

2 tomatoes, skinned and chopped

2 cloves garlic, finely minced

¼ teaspoon thyme

1 bay leaf

12 small potatoes, peeled and cubed

6 carrots, cut into 1½-inch lengths

6 small turnips, peeled and cubed

12 small white onions

1 cup shelled peas or 1 package (10 ounces) frozen

1 cup green beans, cut into ½-inch lengths

1. Preheat oven to 325 degrees.

2. Brown meat on all sides, a few pieces at a time, in oil. Transfer meat to a heavy heatproof casserole.

3. Sprinkle meat with sugar and place casserole over moderately high heat 4 or 5 minutes.

4. Season meat with salt and pepper, sprinkle with flour; cook 5 minutes longer, stirring.

5. Add lamb or beef stock to cover. Add tomatoes, garlic, thyme and bay leaf and bring to a boil.

6. Cover and bake in oven 1 to 1½ hours, until meat is almost tender.

7. Remove meat to another casserole. Strain sauce, skim off excess fat and pour sauce over meat.

8. Add potatoes, carrots, turnips and onions. Cover and bake 25 minutes or until vegetables are almost tender.

9. Add peas and beans and bake 15 minutes. If frozen peas are used, add for last 5 minutes only.

Roast Loin of Pork au Vin Blanc

Yield: 6 to 8 servings

1 loin of pork (6 to 8
    pounds)
4 cloves garlic
  Salt and black pepper
3 sprigs parsley

1 teaspoon thyme
1 crumbled bay leaf
¼ cup olive oil
½ bottle (1⅔ cups) dry
    white wine

1. Wipe pork with a damp cloth.

2. Cut garlic into thin slivers. Make small incisions around ribs and bones of loin and put garlic slivers inside. Sprinkle loin liberally with salt and pepper and place in a baking dish. Add parsley, thyme and bay leaf. Rub loin with oil and pour wine over all. Cover with foil and refrigerate 12 hours or longer. Turn pork occasionally in the wine marinade.

208

3. Preheat oven to 325 degrees.

4. Roast pork 40 minutes a pound, basting occasionally with marinade. When done, roast should be mahogany brown. Remove pork from oven and let set in a warm place about 20 minutes while making sauce.

5. Strain drippings in pan into a large glass measuring cup. Pour or skim off most of fat. Return drippings to roasting pan and add ¾ cup water. Cook on top of stove, stirring to dissolve brown particles that cling to bottom and sides of pan. Pour sauce into a sauce boat and serve separately.

Red Cabbage with Pork

Yield: About 6 servings

¼ pound sliced bacon

2 large onions, sliced

1 clove garlic, finely chopped

3 carrots, finely diced

2 large tart apples, peeled and diced

1 red cabbage, shredded (about 1½ quarts)

1 bay leaf, crumbled

¼ teaspoon nutmeg

⅛ teaspoon allspice

¼ teaspoon black pepper

Salt to taste

2 cups dry red wine

1 loin of pork (5 pounds)

18 peeled chestnuts (see note)

Canned beef broth

1 tablespoon wine vinegar

1. Preheat oven to 325 degrees.

2. Cover bacon with water; bring to a boil, simmer 3 to 5 minutes, drain and dice. Discard water.

3. Place diced bacon in a stainless steel or porcelainized cast-iron casserole and heat to render fat and brown bacon.

4. Add onions and garlic. Cook slowly until tender. Add carrots and cook 3 minutes.

5. Add apples, cabbage, bay leaf, nutmeg, allspice, pepper, salt and wine. Bring to simmer point, stirring occasionally.

6. Brown pork roast in a skillet and place atop the cooking cabbage. Cover tightly and bake in oven at least 3 hours. Allow about 30 minutes' cooking time a pound; the internal temperature should register 185 degrees when done.

7. Add chestnuts to cabbage 1 hour before the end of cooking time. A small quantity of beef broth may be added if dry.

8. To serve, remove roast to a warm platter. Evaporate any excess liquid in the cabbage by boiling; add wine vinegar, correct seasoning and serve as a bed under roast.

Note: To peel chestnuts, make a gash in the flat side of each chestnut. Place in a pan with 1 teaspoon oil and shake until coated. Transfer to a 350-degree oven and heat until shells and inner skin can be removed easily.

Stuffed Fresh Ham

Yield: 15 to 20 servings

1 fresh ham (10 to 14 pounds)

¼ cup butter

1 cup chopped onion

3 cloves garlic, chopped

7 cups soft bread crumbs
(two 1-pound loaves,
crusts removed)

2 large tart apples,
unpeeled and diced

1 cup chopped celery

½ cup chopped parsley

1 tablespoon salt

½ teaspoon black pepper

2 teaspoons sage

1 teaspoon thyme

1 teaspoon grated lemon
rind

1. Have butcher remove bone, leaving a pocket for stuffing, and skin from fresh ham (leg of pork).

2. Preheat oven to 325 degrees.

3. Melt butter in a skillet and sauté onion and garlic until tender but not browned.

4. Mix cooked onion mixture with remaining ingredients in a large bowl. Pack stuffing (it will be dry) into the pocket lightly. Close the opening with skewers and string.

5. Place ham, fat side up, on a rack in a roasting pan. Roast about 35 minutes a pound or until the internal temperature is 185 degrees (5½ to 7½ hours). Serve hot with Madeira sauce (page 253) or cold.

Pork Chops
with Mustard

Yield: 4 servings

2 tablespoons butter
4 loin pork chops, each
    1½ inches thick
Salt and black pepper
1 tablespoon chopped
    shallot
1 tablespoon flour
1 cup chicken broth

2 tablespoons brown sauce
    or canned beef gravy
2 teaspoons prepared mus-
    tard (preferably Dijon
    or Düsseldorf)
2 tablespoons chopped sour
    gherkins or sweet pickles

1. Melt 1 tablespoon butter in a skillet; cook chops on both sides over relatively high heat. Sprinkle chops with salt and pepper. Reduce heat and continue cooking over very low heat until chops are tender. Cook thoroughly until chops are well done, turning occasionally.

2. Transfer chops to a warm platter and keep warm.

3. Pour off all but 1 tablespoon fat from skillet and add shallots. Cook, stirring, until shallots are wilted. Sprinkle with flour and stir. Gradually add broth and brown sauce, stirring with a wire whisk until blended and smooth. Return chops to sauce and continue to cook about 5 minutes a side.

4. Return chops to platter. Add mustard, gherkins or pickles and remaining tablespoon of butter. Swirl sauce around but do not boil. Spoon sauce over the chops and serve hot.

Oven-Barbecued Spareribs

Yield: 4 servings

3 pounds spareribs

½ cup granulated brown
   sugar

1 tablespoon dry mustard

2 teaspoons salt

¼ teaspoon black pepper

¾ teaspoon ginger

½ teaspoon cinnamon

1 can (8 ounces) tomato
   sauce

¾ cup vinegar

1¼ teaspoons Tabasco sauce

2 tablespoons grated onion

1½ cloves garlic, crushed

1. Preheat oven to 350 degrees.

2. Place spareribs on a rack in a shallow pan and roast 45 minutes. Pour off excess fat as it accumulates.

3. Meanwhile, combine sugar and spices in a saucepan; mix well. Add remaining ingredients and bring to a boil over medium heat, stirring occasionally.

4. Pour a third of sauce over ribs and continue to roast 30 minutes. Turn ribs.

5. Pour half the remaining sauce over; roast 1 hour longer, until fully cooked. Brush with extra sauce several times.

Saltimbocca

Yield: 4 servings

8 slices boneless veal cutlet (about 2 pounds), pounded until thin

Salt and black pepper

8 fresh sage leaves

8 thin slices prosciutto (Italian ham)

¼ cup butter

¼ cup Marsala wine

1. Season pounded veal with salt and pepper. Top each piece with sage leaf and then a slice of prosciutto. Secure with toothpicks if necessary.

2. Melt butter in a heavy skillet and brown meat on both sides. Place on a warm platter, ham side up. Add wine to skillet and heat while scraping to loosen all cooked-on bits. When mixture boils, pour it over meat.

Veal Birds

Yield: 6 servings

1½ cups fine soft bread
    crumbs
1½ teaspoons crumbled
    leaf sage
1 egg, lightly beaten
2 tablespoons chopped
    parsley
7 tablespoons butter
    Salt and black pepper
6 oysters
6 thin slices veal (from leg
    as for scaloppine), about
    6 by 3 inches, pounded

2 tablespoons flour
1 tablespoon finely
    chopped shallot
¼ cup dry white wine
½ cup chicken broth
1 pound green noodles,
    cooked and drained
½ cup heavy cream

1. Mix together bread crumbs, sage, egg, parsley, 4 tablespoons butter, melted, and salt and pepper to taste.

2. Wrap each oyster (reserving juice) completely in stuffing and place at one end of each veal slice. Roll up and secure with string, tucking in the sides. Coat veal rolls lightly with the flour seasoned with salt and pepper.

3. Melt remaining butter in a skillet and brown veal rolls on all sides. Add chopped shallot and cook 3 minutes.

4. Add wine, reserved oyster liquid and chicken broth. Bring to a boil; cover and simmer very gently over low heat until veal is tender, about 25 minutes.

5. Arrange rolls on a warm platter. Surround with noodles. Add cream to skillet and heat, stirring. Test for seasoning and pour over rolls.

Stuffed Breast
of Veal

Yield: 10 to 12 servings

1 breast of veal (4 pounds)
1 pound spinach
1 pound ground pork
½ pound mushrooms
2 cups chopped onion
2 cloves garlic, chopped
6 shallots, chopped
2 bay leaves, chopped
½ teaspoon thyme
2 eggs

Salt and black pepper
4 slices white bread, made
   into bread crumbs
Peanut oil
1 carrot, chopped
3 sprigs parsley, chopped
1 sprig rosemary (optional)
1 rib celery, coarsely
   chopped
1 to 2 cups water

1. Have butcher bone and trim the veal breast and reserve bones. Have him slit a pocket in veal.

2. Trim spinach and cook briefly. Drain and press well.

3. Preheat oven to 400 degrees.

220

4. Grind spinach, pork, mushrooms, half the onion, half the garlic, the shallots, half the bay leaves and half the thyme together. In a mixing bowl, combine mixture with eggs, salt, pepper and bread crumbs. Mix with hands and stuff veal breast. Sew up the opening. Sprinkle with salt and pepper. Brush with oil.

5. Line a large roasting pan with veal bones and place the stuffed veal breast on them, boned side up. Scatter remaining onion, garlic, thyme, bay leaf, carrot, parsley, rosemary and celery over veal. Reduce heat to 350 degrees. Cook 30 minutes. Turn breast to other side. Baste frequently. Cook 1½ hours and pour off fat.

6. Add 1 cup water and cover with foil. Continue cooking approximately 1 hour longer, adding water if necessary. Remove foil for last 15 minutes of cooking.

7. Transfer meat to a serving platter and remove string. Strain sauce from pan and heat. Serve separately with sliced veal.

Eleanor's
Veal Madelon

Yield: 8 servings

1 clove garlic, finely minced	2 tablespoons flour
2 tablespoons butter	½ teaspoon salt
2 pounds boneless veal from leg or shoulder, cut into small cubes	¼ teaspoon black pepper
	1 cup boiling chicken broth
	2 strips lemon peel
	½ cup heavy cream

1. In a skillet or a heavy casserole, sauté garlic in butter until lightly browned. Remove garlic and brown veal cubes on all sides.

2. Sprinkle with flour, salt and pepper and brown again. Add broth and lemon peel. Cover and simmer until tender, 25 to 60 minutes, depending on cut of meat. Remove lemon peel.

3. Add cream and reheat.

Veal Loaf

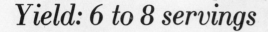

Yield: 6 to 8 servings

1 onion, chopped	2 teaspoons Worcestershire sauce
1 clove garlic, finely chopped	1 teaspoon salt
2 tablespoons butter	¼ teaspoon black pepper
2 pounds ground veal	1 tablespoon lemon juice
2 cups cooked rice	1 teaspoon rosemary
2 eggs, lightly beaten	2 tablespoons chopped parsley
¾ cup heavy cream	8 strips bacon
1 green pepper, diced	

1. Preheat oven to 350 degrees.

2. Sauté onion and garlic in butter until tender and place in a bowl with remaining ingredients except bacon. Mix well but lightly.

3. Pile mixture into 9-by-5-by-3-inch loaf pan. Top with bacon strips and bake 1½ hours.

Jellied Tongue Loaf

Yield: 10 to 12 servings

2 envelopes unflavored
    gelatin
½ cup cold water
1½ cups boiling beef broth
¼ cup mayonnaise
2 teaspoons Dijon or
    Düsseldorf mustard
½ cup milk
⅓ cup vinegar
2 tablespoons chili sauce

1 teaspoon Worcester-
    shire sauce
3 cups ground cooked
    smoked beef tongue
⅓ cup finely diced sweet
    pickles
2 hard-cooked eggs, sliced
2 sweet pickles, sliced
    lengthwise
Salad greens and cherry
    tomatoes

1. Soften gelatin in cold water. Add to boiling broth and stir
to dissolve. Cool.

2. Add mayonnaise, mustard, milk, vinegar, chili sauce and Worcestershire. Mix well and chill until mixture starts to thicken.

3. Add tongue and diced pickles; mix well.

4. Rinse 1½-quart ring mold or 9-by-5-by-3-inch loaf pan with cold water. Arrange sliced eggs and pickles in bottom of mold or pan. Spoon in the meat mixture. Chill until firm.

5. Unmold loaf onto salad greens and garnish with cherry tomatoes.

Oxtail Ragout

Yield: 8 servings

4 oxtails

Flour for dredging

Salt and black pepper

¼ cup peanut oil

1 bay leaf

½ teaspoon thyme

2 ribs celery, chopped

1 carrot, chopped

1 large onion, chopped

2 cloves garlic, crushed

1½ cups dry red wine

2½ cups beef broth

1 tomato, skinned
   and coarsely chopped

2 carrots, cut into strips

1½ cups quartered peeled
   turnips

1 green pepper, cut into
   1-inch cubes

3 tablespoons butter

1. Cut oxtails into 2-inch lengths or have them cut by butcher.

2. Preheat oven to 350 degrees.

3. Dredge oxtails in flour seasoned with salt and pepper.

4. Heat oil in a large heavy skillet and brown oxtails well.

5. Arrange oxtails in a heavy casserole. Add bay leaf, thyme, celery, chopped carrot, chopped onion and garlic. Add wine and beef broth; bring to a boil. Add chopped tomato and cover. Bake 2 hours.

6. When oxtails are fork tender, remove them and keep warm. Strain sauce thoroughly.

7. Meanwhile, cook carrot strips and turnips in salted water to cover about 10 minutes. Do not overcook. Drain and toss carrots, turnips and green pepper cubes in hot butter. Add vegetables to sauce and simmer until tender. Add oxtails and heat. Serve with noodles.

Veal Kidneys
with Celery

Yield: 4 servings

4 tablespoons butter

2 tablespoons finely
  chopped shallots

1 cup finely chopped celery

4 small veal kidneys, cored
  and cut into cubes

¼ pound mushrooms, sliced

2 tablespoons finely
  chopped parsley

½ cup dry red wine

¼ teaspoon dry mustard

1 cup canned beef gravy

Salt and black pepper

1. Melt butter in a heavy skillet and sauté shallots and celery until tender.

2. Add kidney pieces and cook quickly until browned and tender, about 5 minutes. Add mushrooms, parsley, wine mixed with mustard, and brown gravy. Season to taste with salt and pepper and cook 3 minutes.

Eggs, Cheese and Sauces

Fresh Corn Scramble

Yield: 6 servings

6 strips bacon

1 cup fresh corn kernels,
    cut from cob

¼ cup milk

6 eggs, beaten

¾ teaspoon salt

⅛ teaspoon black pepper

6 slices buttered toast

6 tablespoons shredded
    sharp Cheddar cheese

1. Fry bacon until crisp. Remove bacon and all but 2 tablespoons drippings from skillet. Add corn and cook until golden brown, 3 to 5 minutes.

2. Add milk and simmer 2 minutes. Combine eggs with salt and pepper and stir into corn. Cook, stirring with a fork, until eggs are just set.

3. Spoon over toast slices, sprinkle with cheese and place under preheated broiler just long enough to melt cheese. Top each with a strip of bacon.

Mrs. Shaw's Chakchouka

Yield: 4 servings

3 links Italian sweet
    sausages, cut into
    1-inch slices
2 tablespoons olive oil
2 onions, finely chopped
2 cloves garlic, minced
1 green pepper, diced

1 tomato, skinned
    and diced
2 potatoes, peeled
    and diced
1 cup water
Salt and black pepper
3 eggs, lightly beaten

1. Sauté sausage pieces in a skillet until browned.

2. Add olive oil, onions and garlic and cook 3 minutes. Add green pepper, tomato and potatoes and cook 2 minutes longer. Add water and allow mixture to simmer, uncovered, until potato is tender. Season with salt and pepper.

3. Stir in eggs and continue to cook, stirring, until eggs are done, about 2 minutes.

Eggs in Tomato Shells

Yield: 4 servings

4 medium-size firm, ripe
   tomatoes
  Salt and black pepper
4 teaspoons chopped fresh
   basil or 2 teaspoons
   chopped fresh tarragon

4 teaspoons butter
4 large eggs
2 tablespoons freshly grated
   Parmesan cheese
4 large toast rounds, buttered
Watercress

1. Preheat oven to 350 degrees.

2. Cut off a small slice from top of each tomato. Run a paring knife around the inner rim of the tomato and carefully scoop out pulp to make a hollow shell or case.

3. Sprinkle insides of cases with salt and turn upside down on a rack to drain. Place tomatoes right side up and sprinkle again with salt and pepper. Divide basil or tarragon equally among cases; add 1 teaspoon butter to each case and break 1 egg into each.

4. Place tomatoes in a buttered dish and bake 20 to 25 minutes. Do not let yolks become firm. Sprinkle with Parmesan and run tomatoes quickly under broiler. Serve on warm buttered toast rounds. Garnish with watercress.

Scrambled Eggs with Chives

Yield: 2 servings

4 eggs
¼ cup sour cream
Salt and black pepper
  to taste

¼ teaspoon cinnamon
1 tablespoon minced chives
3 tablespoons butter
2 slices buttered toast

1. Break eggs into a mixing bowl and add sour cream, salt, pepper, cinnamon and chives. Beat lightly with a fork.

2. Melt butter in a skillet and add egg mixture. Cook slowly, stirring around bottom and sides with a rubber spatula. Serve on buttered toast.

Piperade with Ham
(A type of omelet with ham)

Yield: 6 servings

¼ cup ham fat, cut into
    cubes, or 2 tablespoons
    bacon fat or butter

2 medium-size onions

3 to 5 cloves garlic

½ bay leaf

2 large tomatoes, skinned
    and chopped

½ teaspoon thyme

Salt and black pepper
    to taste

7 tablespoons butter

12 thin slices ham

12 eggs

Parsley sprigs

1. Place ham fat in a large skillet and cook until rendered of liquid fat.

2. Meanwhile, peel onions and slice in half. Cut each half into paper-thin slices. Add to skillet.

3. Chop garlic cloves. Top with bay leaf and continue chopping until bay leaf is finely chopped. Add to skillet.

234

4. Add tomatoes, thyme, salt and pepper. Cook, stirring occasionally, until sauce thickens, about 15 minutes.

5. Heat 3 tablespoons butter in a large skillet and cook ham briefly.

6. Beat eggs and season with salt and pepper. Add to sauce. Cook, stirring, until thickened; stir in remaining butter.

7. Arrange 2 slices ham on each of 6 plates. Spoon piperade over ham. Garnish with parsley sprigs.

Eggs with Sauce Gribiche

Yield: 6 servings

1 teaspoon minced parsley

1 teaspoon minced onion

½ teaspoon thyme

1 clove garlic, minced

2 teaspoons Dijon or
    Düsseldorf mustard

1 egg yolk

Salt and black pepper

2 tablespoons wine vinegar

1½ cups olive or salad oil

¾ cup diced, seeded
    skinned tomatoes

6 hard-cooked eggs, halved

2 tablespoons minced chives

1. Place parsley, onion, thyme, garlic, mustard, egg yolk, salt, pepper and vinegar in a mixing bowl. Beat with a whisk and start adding oil. Add slowly, beating rapidly, until sauce begins to thicken. Oil may then be added in a thicker stream. When mixture is thick and smooth, it is ready.

2. Stir in tomatoes. Spoon the sauce over egg halves and sprinkle with chives.

Mushroom Soufflé

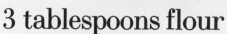

Yield: 4 to 6 servings

½ pound mushrooms, diced
3½ tablespoons butter
   Salt and black pepper
⅛ teaspoon nutmeg

3 tablespoons flour
1 cup milk
4 egg yolks
5 egg whites

1. Preheat oven to 400 degrees.

2. Sauté mushrooms in 1 tablespoon butter 2 to 3 minutes. Puree mushrooms. Season with salt, pepper and nutmeg.

3. Melt remaining butter in a pan; blend in flour. Gradually stir in milk. Bring to a boil, stirring. Beat in egg yolks, one at a time. Fold in puree. Taste for seasoning.

4. Beat egg whites until stiff but not dry. Stir half the whites into mushroom mixture. Fold in remaining whites.

5. Pour into greased 6-cup soufflé dish. Place in oven; immediately reduce heat to 375 degrees and bake 35 minutes. Serve immediately.

Alaska King Crab Soufflé

Yield: 4 to 6 servings

¼ cup butter
¼ cup flour
1 cup milk
4 eggs, separated
1 cup king crab meat
　　(frozen or canned),
　　cut into chunks

1 teaspoon onion juice or
　　finely grated onion
¼ teaspoon black pepper
2 tablespoons chopped
　　parsley
½ teaspoon salt

1. Preheat oven to 325 degrees.

2. Melt butter in a small pan. Blend in flour; gradually stir in milk. Cook over low heat, stirring, until thickened.

3. Remove from heat. Beat in egg yolks, one at a time. Fold in crab meat, onion juice, pepper and parsley. Beat egg whites with salt until stiff but not dry; fold into the crab meat mixture.

4. Turn mixture into a 1½-quart soufflé dish greased on the bottom only. With a teaspoon, circle the mixture about 1 inch deep about 1 inch from the sides.

5. Bake 50 to 60 minutes or until delicately browned and well puffed and a knife inserted halfway between center and outside comes out clean.

Bean Rarebit

Yield: 4 servings

2 cups grated sharp
   Cheddar cheese
1 can (No. 300) red kidney
   beans (2 cups), drained
   and rinsed

½ cup diced green pepper
6 stuffed green olives, sliced
1 tablespoon Worcestershire
   sauce
Toast or cooked rice

1. Melt cheese over hot water or in a chafing dish.

2. Stir in the remaining ingredients except toast or rice and heat, stirring. Serve over toast or rice.

Hearts of Palm au Gratin

Yield: 8 to 10 servings

3 cans (14 ounces each)
   hearts of palm,
   drained (see note)
6 tablespoons butter
4 tablespoons flour
1½ cups milk
   Dash of Tabasco sauce

½ cup grated Swiss or
   Gruyère cheese
½ cup heavy cream
   Salt and black pepper
½ cup freshly grated
   Parmesan cheese

1. Preheat oven to 400 degrees.

2. Cut drained hearts of palm into 1-inch pieces; place in a greased shallow heatproof dish.

3. Melt 4 tablespoons butter in a heavy saucepan and stir in flour. Cook over low heat 2 or 3 minutes.

4. Heat milk to just below boiling point. Add to roux all at once, stirring vigorously with spoon or wire whisk.

5. Simmer 5 minutes. Add Tabasco, Swiss cheese, cream and seasonings. Stir until cheese is melted. Pour over hearts of palm.

6. Melt remaining 2 tablespoons butter and brush top with a thin layer of butter. Sprinkle with Parmesan cheese and bake 10 to 12 minutes, until glazed.

Note: You may substitute 3 packages (10 ounces each) frozen artichoke hearts, if desired. Cook according to package directions and drain well.

Bacon and Cheese Pudding

Yield: 6 servings

6 slices day-old bread

¼ pound bacon, diced

¾ cup finely chopped onion

4 eggs

¾ cup shredded Cheddar
     cheese

3 cups milk

½ teaspoon nutmeg

Salt and black pepper

1. Preheat oven to 350 degrees.

2. Trim off and discard crusts of bread and cut each slice into quarters. Arrange quarters in a shallow 5-cup baking dish.

3. Cook bacon in a skillet until golden brown. Using a slotted spoon, remove bacon and sprinkle over bread in dish.

4. Pour off all but 2 tablespoons drippings from the skillet and add onion. Cook, stirring, until wilted. Add contents of the skillet to bread and bacon.

5. Beat eggs lightly and stir in cheese, milk and seasonings. Pour mixture over bread and bacon and place baking dish in a larger pan. Pour hot water around baking dish. Bake 45 minutes or until firm.

Cream Cheese Sauce

Yield: About 1¼ cups

8 ounces cream cheese
2 eggs
2 tablespoons lemon juice

¼ teaspoon salt
⅛ teaspoon white pepper

1. Soften cream cheese to room temperature and beat in eggs, one at a time.

2. Beat in remaining ingredients and place in top of a double boiler over hot, but not boiling, water. Cook, stirring, until sauce is thick and fluffy. *For vegetables and fish.*

Mayonnaise

Yield: About 1½ cups

½ teaspoon dry mustard

1 teaspoon cold water

2 egg yolks

  Salt to taste

  Pinch of cayenne pepper

3 tablespoons wine
  vinegar or lemon
  juice

1¼ cups peanut or
  vegetable oil

1. Place mustard in a mixing bowl and add water to make a paste. Let stand 10 minutes.

2. Add yolks, salt, pepper and half the vinegar. Start beating with a whisk, rotary beater or electric beater, gradually adding peanut oil. Continue beating, adding remaining vinegar and oil alternately until all ingredients are used.

3. Taste for seasoning and add more salt, cayenne or vinegar if desired.

Rémoulade Sauce

Yield: 2¼ cups

2 cups homemade
   mayonnaise (page 244)
2 tablespoons finely
   chopped scallions
1 teaspoon anchovy paste

2 teaspoons Dijon mustard
1 hard-cooked egg, chopped
1 tablespoon chopped
   capers
½ teaspoon tarragon

Blend all ingredients and chill well. *For shellfish.*

Anchovy Butter

Yield: About 1¼ cups

½ pound sweet butter
1 can (2 ounces) anchovies

Juice of 1 lemon

1. Melt butter in a saucepan without letting it brown.
2. Drain anchovies and chop them in a small bowl. Add to butter. Add lemon juice. Stir and serve warm. *For fish.*

Celery Sauce

Yield: 4 servings

1 cup chopped celery	2½ tablespoons butter
Salt	2½ tablespoons flour
½ cup (approximately) milk	Black pepper
	Cayenne pepper to taste
½ cup heavy cream	¼ teaspoon grated nutmeg

1. Place celery in a small saucepan and add water barely to cover. Add salt to taste and simmer about 5 minutes.

2. Drain liquid from celery into measuring cup. Add enough milk to make 1 cup, then add cream. Reserve cooked celery.

3. Melt butter in a saucepan and stir in flour. Add milk mixture, stirring vigorously with a whisk. When mixture is thickened and smooth, continue cooking 15 minutes or longer, stirring occasionally with whisk. Add celery and remaining ingredients. Serve hot. *For fish.*

Fresh Tomato Sauce

Yield: About 2 cups

1 tablespoon butter
½ cup finely chopped onion
1 clove garlic, finely minced
2 cups chopped skinned
   tomatoes

½ teaspoon thyme
1 bay leaf
Salt and black pepper
   to taste

1. Heat butter in a saucepan and cook onion and garlic until onion is translucent.

2. Add remaining ingredients and cook, stirring occasionally, about 15 minutes. Sauce may be used "as is" or strained. *For omelets, pasta, fish, chicken, casseroles and meat loaves.*

Mustard Sauce

Yield: About 1½ cups

1 teaspoon dry mustard	¼ cup wine vinegar
1 cup water	1 teaspoon grated
1 tablespoon cornstarch	horseradish
2 teaspoons sugar	2 egg yolks, lightly beaten
½ teaspoon salt	1 tablespoon cold butter

1. Place mustard in top of a double boiler and add just enough water to make a paste. Let stand 10 minutes. Add cornstarch, sugar, salt and remaining water. Heat, stirring, until thick; cook about 1 minute.

2. Off heat, stir in vinegar, horseradish and egg yolks. Continue cooking, stirring, until sauce thickens more. Do not overcook or sauce may curdle. Remove from heat, swirl in cold butter and serve immediately. *For boiled beef and pan-fried trout.*

Mushroom Sauce

Yield: 3½ cups

¼ cup butter
2 tablespoons chopped
   shallots
½ pound mushrooms,
   finely chopped
5 tablespoons flour

1½ cups milk
1 cup heavy cream
1 cup grated Swiss cheese
Salt and black pepper
   to taste

1. Melt butter in a saucepan and add shallots. Cook briefly, stirring, and add mushrooms. Cook until mushrooms have wilted and most of liquid has evaporated.

2. Sprinkle with flour and add milk and cream gradually, stirring vigorously. When sauce is thick, remove from heat and stir in cheese, salt and pepper. *For fish, chicken, veal and meat loaves.*

249

Paprika Sauce

Yield: 1½ cups

2 tablespoons butter

3 tablespoons chopped
   onion

2 teaspoons paprika

1 tablespoon flour

½ teaspoon thyme

½ cup chicken broth

½ cup heavy cream

2 teaspoons lemon juice

Salt and black pepper
   to taste

1 teaspoon cognac

¼ cup sour cream

1. Melt 1 tablespoon butter in a small saucepan and cook onion until wilted. Sprinkle with paprika, flour and thyme, stirring. Stir in the chicken broth, using a wire whisk, and simmer about 3 minutes.

2. Add cream and bring to a boil. Add lemon juice, salt, pepper and cognac. Strain through a sieve. Return to heat and stir in remaining butter and sour cream. Reheat but do not boil. *For chicken, veal and fish.*

Hollandaise Sauce

Yield: 1½ cups

8 egg yolks	Salt and black pepper
6 tablespoons hot water	½ pound butter
4 tablespoons lemon juice	

1. In a saucepan, beat yolks with a wire whisk until they are thick and pale in color. Add hot water, lemon juice and salt and pepper to taste and beat hard.

2. In another saucepan, heat butter just to bubbling. Pour it slowly into egg mixture, beating rapidly.

3. Place sauce over very low heat and cook, stirring constantly, until properly thickened. Do not overcook or it will curdle. To restore slightly curdled sauce, add 2 tablespoons cold light cream and beat quickly, off the heat. *For vegetables and eggs benedict.*

251

Quick Hollandaise Sauce

Yield: ⅓ cup

2 egg yolks

1½ tablespoons lemon juice

⅛ teaspoon salt

Pinch of cayenne pepper

⅓ cup butter, melted, hot
but not browned

Blend yolks, juice, salt and cayenne. Turn blender to low speed and gradually pour in butter. Serve immediately or keep warm in a pan of hot water. *For vegetables.*

Lemon Butter Sauce

Yield: ¾ cup

½ cup sweet butter

2 teaspoons lemon juice

2 drops Tabasco sauce

2 drops Worcestershire sauce

1 tablespoon chopped
parsley

Melt butter and add remaining ingredients. Serve warm. *For fish, shellfish and vegetables.*

Madeira Sauce

Yield: About 1 quart

Ham skin
Ham bone or veal knuckle
2 tablespoons butter
6 shallots, finely chopped
2 tablespoons flour
1 cup dry red wine

1 can (10½ ounces) beef
   gravy
½ cup currant jelly
¼ cup Madeira
2 tablespoons chopped
   parsley

1. Cover ham skin and bone with cold water. Bring to a boil, cover and simmer 3 hours. Strain broth. Reduce broth by boiling rapidly until there are 2 cups.

2. Melt butter in a skillet and sauté shallots until tender but not browned. Sprinkle with flour and cook, stirring, 1 minute.

3. Stir in broth, red wine, gravy and jelly. Bring to a boil, stirring, and simmer 10 minutes. Stir in Madeira and parsley. *For ham.*

Sauce Robert

Yield: About 1 cup

¼ cup dry white wine
1 bay leaf
2 tablespoons finely
    chopped shallots
1½ teaspoons chopped onion
1 clove garlic, minced
½ teaspoon thyme
½ cup tomato puree
½ cup chicken broth
½ cup brown sauce or
    canned beef gravy

½ cup thinly sliced
    cornichons (sour
    pickles)
2 tablespoons chopped
    parsley
Beef stock
1 tablespoon Dijon or
    Düsseldorf mustard
2 tablespoons butter

1. Combine wine, bay leaf, shallots, onion, garlic and thyme in a saucepan and simmer until wine is reduced to about 2 tablespoons. Add tomato puree, chicken broth and brown sauce and cook 20 minutes, stirring occasionally.

2. Remove bay leaf and add cornichons and parsley. If sauce seems too thick, thin with beef broth. Bring sauce to a boil. Remove from heat.

3. Stir in mustard and swirl in butter. Do not cook further but serve hot. *For broiled chops, chicken and steaks.*

Sauce Chien

Yield: About 1 cup

⅓ cup lime juice
¼ cup vegetable oil
½ clove garlic, minced
   Salt and black pepper
3 tablespoons chopped
   parsley

1 tablespoon finely
   chopped scallion
1 teaspoon thinly sliced
   hot green peppers
Cayenne pepper

Combine all ingredients and beat with a fork or wire whisk to blend. *For broiled chicken, fish, chops and steak.*

Sauce Belle Aurore

Yield: About 4 cups

2 cups unstrained
  fresh tomato sauce
  (page 247)
6 tablespoons butter
3 tablespoons flour
1¾ cups chicken broth

¾ cup cooking stock
  from a boiled ham
  (see note)
1 cup heavy cream
¼ cup port wine

1. Prepare tomato sauce and set aside.

2. Melt half the butter in a saucepan and stir in flour, using a wire whisk. Add chicken broth and ham stock, stirring vigorously with a wire whisk. When mixture is thickened and smooth, continue cooking about 1 hour, stirring occasionally.

3. Add tomato sauce and stir. Cook 5 minutes. Stir in heavy cream and strain through a sieve or food mill.

4. Return sauce to a saucepan, bring to a boil and swirl in remaining butter. Add port; heat thoroughly and serve hot. *For ham, chicken and veal.*

Note: If ham stock is not available, use an additional ¾ cup chicken broth.

Caper or Horseradish Sauce

Yield: 1½ cups

3 tablespoons butter
3 tablespoons flour

1½ cups boiling beef stock
Capers or horseradish

1. Melt butter in a saucepan; add flour and stir with a wire whisk until blended.
2. Add boiling beef stock all at once, stirring vigorously until the mixture is thickened and smooth. Season with capers or horseradish. *For boiled beef, tongue or corned beef.*

Paprika
Sour Cream Sauce

Yield: 4 servings

1 teaspoon dry mustard	⅛ teaspoon black pepper
1 teaspoon water	1 egg yolk, beaten
2 teaspoons sugar	¼ cup vinegar
2 teaspoons flour	1 tablespoon melted butter
1 teaspoon salt	½ cup sour cream
1 teaspoon paprika	

1. Mix mustard with water; let stand 10 minutes for flavor to develop.

2. Combine mustard with sugar, flour, salt, paprika and pepper in top of a double boiler or in a saucepan. Beat in egg yolk and vinegar. Cook, stirring, over hot water until mixture is smooth and thick, about 7 minutes. Blend in butter.

3. Cool sauce and fold in sour cream. *For cold fried chicken or cold veal cutlet.*

Orange-Soy Marinade

Yield: 2 cups

1 cup imported soy sauce
1 cup orange marmalade
2 cloves garlic, minced

1 tablespoon finely chopped
fresh ginger
¼ teaspoon black pepper

Combine ingredients. Allow meat to marinate a few hours or overnight in refrigerator. *For pork cubes and chicken.*

Garlic Marinade

Yield: About 3 cups

3 cloves garlic
¼ teaspoon thyme
¼ teaspoon marjoram
¼ teaspoon oregano
½ teaspoon Worcestershire

⅓ cup olive oil
1 cup dry red wine
1 onion, sliced
1 bay leaf
Salt and black pepper

Combine ingredients. Allow meat to marinate several hours or overnight in the refrigerator. *For pork, beef and lamb.*

Sparerib Marinade

Yield: About 1½ cups

6 tablespoons olive oil
2 tablespoons wine vinegar
  Salt and black pepper
    to taste
1 clove garlic, minced
1 teaspoon Dijon or Düssel-
    dorf mustard

½ teaspoon crumbled
    rosemary
1 tablespoon soy sauce,
    preferably imported
½ cup dry red wine

Mix all the ingredients together and use to marinate 4 to 5 pounds spareribs for several hours.

Rice, Grains, Beans and Potatoes

Shirin Polo
(Orange-Almond Rice)

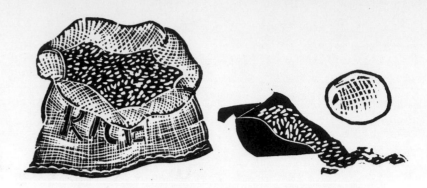

Yield: 10 servings

2½ cups rice
Salt
8 tablespoons butter
1 cup sliced blanched
   almonds

1 cup candied orange peel,
   cut in 1-inch slivers
½ teaspoon whole saffron

1. Wash rice several times in warm water and soak in cold salted water at least 2 hours, overnight if possible. Drain rice and add with 2 tablespoons salt to 2 quarts boiling water. Boil 15 minutes or until tender. Pour rice and water into a strainer and rinse with lukewarm water.

2. While rice is cooking, heat 4 tablespoons butter in a skillet and sauté almonds.

3. Heat remaining butter in another skillet and cook orange peel very slowly 10 minutes.

4. Mix rice, almonds and orange peel in a saucepan. Add ¼ cup water, cover with a towel and a lid and cook over low heat ½ hour. When ready to serve, sprinkle with saffron dissolved in 3 tablespoons water and mix.

Note: Good with any poultry or pork.

Cumin Rice

Yield: 6 servings

½ cup chopped onion	1 tablespoon soy sauce
¼ cup diced green pepper	¾ teaspoon salt
1 cup rice	¾ teaspoon ground cumin
2 tablespoons bacon fat	seeds
2½ cups beef broth	

1. In a large saucepan, cook onion, green pepper and rice in bacon fat until golden brown, stirring frequently.

2. Add remaining ingredients and bring to a boil, stirring. Cover tightly; reduce heat and simmer 20 minutes.

Rice and Lentil Casserole

Yield: 8 servings

⅔ cup lentils, washed

¼ cup butter

5 ribs celery, diced

1 onion, chopped

1 cup rice

2 cups chicken broth

1 can (No. 2) tomatoes

1 teaspoon salt

1½ tablespoons sugar

⅓ cup buttered bread crumbs

¼ cup freshly grated
      Parmesan cheese

1. Soak lentils overnight. Simmer slowly in the same water until tender, about 2 hours.

2. Melt butter in a saucepan and sauté celery and onion until tender. Add rice and cook 3 to 5 minutes longer. Add broth and cook until rice is dry.

3. Preheat oven to 350 degrees.

4. Add tomatoes, salt and sugar to rice and vegetables. Drain cooked lentils and add along with ¼ cup of lentil liquid. Pour into greased 2-quart baking dish.

5. Top with buttered crumbs and bake 30 minutes. Sprinkle with cheese and brown under broiler. Let set 10 minutes before serving.

Mexican Rice

Yield: 8 servings

½ cup ground raw pork

3 tablespoons peanut oil

2 chorizos (Spanish sausages)

¼ cup chopped onion

2 tablespoons chopped green pepper

1 clove garlic, finely minced

2 cups rice

4 cups boiling chicken broth

½ teaspoon leaf saffron, crumbled

Salt to taste

1. Cook pork in oil until it loses color. Slice chorizos and add to pork along with onion, pepper and garlic. Continue cooking about 10 minutes, stirring.

2. Add rice, chicken broth, saffron and salt and simmer until rice is tender. Cover and let stand until ready to serve.

Arroz con Gandules
(Rice with Pigeon Peas)

Yield: 4 servings

3 tablespoons diced
  salt pork

2 green peppers, chopped

2 tomatoes, skinned and
  chopped

1 onion, finely chopped

2 cloves garlic, chopped

1 tablespoon capers

2 cups long-grain rice

1 teaspoon salt

1 tablespoon achiote (see note)

1 pound cooked fresh pigeon
  peas or 1 can peas

3 cups water

1. Sauté salt pork until most of fat has been rendered. Add peppers, tomatoes, onion and garlic and cook 5 minutes.

2. Add remaining ingredients. Bring to a boil and simmer, covered, until all the liquid has been absorbed (about 15 minutes). Continue cooking, stirring occasionally to prevent sticking, until rice is cooked and very dry and fluffy.

Note: Achiote is a spice that gives a yellow color to the rice.

Rice
with Herbs

Yield: 6 to 8 servings

4 tablespoons butter

1 tablespoon chopped onion

1 cup rice

½ teaspoon thyme

1 bay leaf

2 sprigs parsley

2 drops Tabasco sauce

3 cups chicken broth

1. Preheat oven to 400 degrees.

2. Melt 2 tablespoons butter in a saucepan and add onion. Cook, stirring, until onion is translucent. Add rice; cook 3 minutes longer. Add thyme, bay leaf, parsley, Tabasco and broth. Bring to a boil, cover tightly and transfer to oven. Bake 20 minutes or until rice is tender and fluffy.

3. Remove the cover, dot rice with remaining butter and stir lightly. Remove bay leaf and parsley. Serve immediately.

Bulgur Jambalaya

Yield: 6 servings

1¼ cups bulgur
2½ cups water
½ teaspoon salt
8 ounces sausage meat
1 cup diced ham
½ cup chopped onion
½ cup chopped green pepper

¾ cup chopped celery
3½ cups chicken broth
2 tablespoons chopped parsley
¼ teaspoon thyme
⅛ teaspoon cloves
¼ teaspoon chili powder
Salt and black pepper

1. Place bulgur, water and salt in saucepan. Cover, bring to a boil and simmer 15 minutes. Remove from heat.

2. In a heavy skillet, sauté sausage, ham, onion, pepper and celery until lightly browned. Add cooked bulgur and the remaining ingredients. Cover; bring to a boil. Simmer, stirring occasionally, until mixture is thickened, about 45 minutes.

268

Wild Rice Casserole

Yield: 4 servings

1½ cups wild rice	¼ cup chopped green pepper
4 strips bacon, diced	½ cup chopped heart of
¼ pound mushrooms,	celery
sliced	½ cup chicken broth
¾ cup chopped onion	Chopped scallions

1. Place wild rice in a colander and rinse under cold water. Put in a large saucepan and add boiling water to cover. Let stand 20 minutes; drain. Repeat. Continue to add water and drain until rice is almost tender, about 3 times.

2. Preheat oven to 350 degrees.

3. Cook bacon until golden brown. Pour off all but 2 tablespoons drippings. Add mushrooms, onion, green pepper and celery. Cook until vegetables are wilted. Spoon mixture onto rice. Add broth and cover. Bake 30 minutes, stirring twice. Serve sprinkled with chopped scallions.

Baked Wild Rice with Carrots

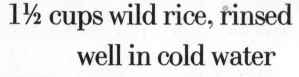

Yield: 6 servings

1½ cups wild rice, rinsed well in cold water	1 onion, finely chopped
2½ cups water or broth	1 cup sliced mushrooms
2 teaspoons salt	1 cup finely grated carrots
4 strips bacon, diced	½ cup light cream
	1 egg

1. Combine rice, water and salt in a large saucepan. Bring to a boil and cook vigorously 10 minutes. Remove pan from heat and cover. Let stand 20 minutes to absorb water.

2. Cook bacon and drain. Reserve drippings.

3. Preheat oven to 325 degrees.

4. Cook onion and mushrooms in bacon drippings until onions are wilted. Stir in bacon, wild rice and grated carrots.

5. Beat cream and egg together and stir into rice mixture. Cover and bake ½ hour in a buttered 1½-quart casserole.

6. Stir with a fork and continue baking 15 minutes. Stir once more and bake, uncovered, 15 minutes longer.

Barley Casserole

Yield: 6 to 8 servings

½ cup butter
2 onions, chopped
¾ pound mushrooms, sliced
1½ cups pearl barley

1 jar (4 ounces) pimentos, coarsely chopped
¼ teaspoon salt
⅛ teaspoon pepper
3 cups chicken broth

1. Preheat oven to 350 degrees.

2. Melt butter in a skillet. Sauté onions until tender but not browned. Add mushrooms and cook 2 minutes.

3. Add barley and cook until delicately browned. Place in a 1½-quart casserole. Add pimentos, salt, pepper and 2 cups broth. Cover and bake 45 minutes. Add remaining broth and cook 30 minutes longer.

Frijoles
(Mexican Beans)

Yield: 4 to 6 servings

2 cups pink, pinto or	½ bay leaf
kidney beans	Salt to taste
5½ cups lukewarm water	½ cup bacon fat or lard
1 onion	

1. Rinse beans but do not soak them. Place in saucepan and add water, onion and bay leaf. Cover and simmer until beans are wrinkled. Stir occasionally.

2. Add salt and continue cooking until beans are thoroughly tender. If necessary, add more water, a little at a time, as beans cook. When beans are nearly done, mash a few to thicken. Continue cooking, stirring frequently, until done. Add bacon fat; cook 10 minutes longer or until beans have desired thickness.

Baked Beans

Yield: 6 servings

½ pound salt pork, diced
1 pound white Michigan
   or pea beans
½ cup brown sugar
½ cup dark molasses

1 teaspoon dry mustard
1 teaspoon salt
1 onion, studded with
   2 cloves

1. Place pork and beans in a large mixing bowl and add water to reach 1 inch over top of the beans. Let stand overnight.

2. Pour into a 3-quart saucepan. Add remaining ingredients and bring to a boil. Simmer, partly covered, 1 hour.

3. Preheat oven to 350 degrees.

4. Discard onion; pour beans into an earthenware crock or bean pot. Cover and bake 2½ hours. Look at the beans occasionally; if they are cooking too fast, reduce heat.

Pinto Bean Pot

Yield: 8 servings

1 pound (2 cups) pinto
  beans
6 cups water
1 tablespoon oil
½ cup salt pork cubes
1 cup chopped onion
2 cloves garlic
1 teaspoon salt
¼ teaspoon black pepper

½ teaspoon oregano
½ teaspoon cumin
3 teaspoons chili powder
1 can (8 ounces) tomato
  sauce
Onion and green pepper
  rings
⅓ cup shredded provolone
  cheese

1. Wash beans. Cover with water; soak overnight. Place in a deep kettle with oil and cook, covered, until tender, about 2 hours.

2. Meanwhile, sauté salt pork until crisp; remove bits and reserve. Sauté onion in drippings until tender. Mash garlic with salt and add.

274

3. Preheat oven to 325 degrees.

4. Add seasonings, tomato sauce and reserved pork to onion. Add 1 cup liquid from cooked beans. Cook 5 minutes. Combine sauce with beans.

5. Turn bean mixture into a casserole or bean pot; cover and bake 2 hours. Check seasoning.

6. Garnish with onion and green pepper rings and shreds of provolone cheese.

Country-Style Beans

Yield: 6 to 8 servings

1 pound dry navy or pea
   beans, washed

2 teaspoons salt

½ teaspoon black pepper

1 clove garlic, chopped

1 bay leaf

6 strips bacon

2 onions, chopped

1 green pepper, chopped

3 tomatoes, skinned and
   chopped

½ teaspoon oregano

¼ cup chopped parsley

1. Soak beans overnight. Simmer beans in water to cover with salt, pepper, garlic and bay leaf until just tender.

2. Preheat oven to 350 degrees.

3. Fry bacon until crisp; remove and reserve. Sauté onions in drippings; add green pepper and tomatoes and cook 5 minutes longer. Stir in oregano and parsley.

4. Drain beans and reserve liquid. Mix beans thoroughly with all other ingredients, including crumbled bacon.

5. Place in a casserole, adding bean liquid to cover. Bake 1 hour or more, adding liquid if necessary.

Green Noodles and Cheese

Yield: 6 servings

8 ounces narrow green spinach noodles, cooked al dente and drained

6 to 8 ounces Swiss cheese, finely grated

1 egg, lightly beaten

1 cup light cream

2 tablespoons freshly grated Parmesan cheese

1 tablespoon butter

1. Preheat oven to 375 degrees.

2. In a small baking dish (about 6-cup size), layer cooked noodles with grated Swiss cheese.

3. Combine egg with cream and pour over noodles and cheese. Top with Parmesan and dot with butter. Bake until bubbly hot, about 25 minutes.

Potato Croquettes

Yield: 4 servings

5 Idaho potatoes

2 tablespoons butter

½ teaspoon nutmeg

   Salt and black pepper

⅓ cup grated Swiss cheese

1 egg yolk

½ cup flour

1 egg, lightly beaten

1 teaspoon vegetable oil

2 tablespoons water

1 cup bread crumbs

¼ cup freshly grated

      Parmesan cheese

Oil for deep-frying

1. Preheat oven to 400 degrees.

2. Bake potatoes until tender, 45 minutes. Remove flesh and sieve or rice into a heavy casserole. Place over low heat.

3. Beat in butter, nutmeg, salt, pepper, Swiss cheese and egg yolk until mixture leaves sides of pan. Cool, then chill. Shape into 18 balls. Dredge in flour.

4. Combine beaten egg with salt, pepper, oil and water. Dip balls into mixture.

278

5. Combine crumbs with Parmesan cheese and roll balls in this mixture. Deep-fry, a few at a time, at 360 degrees until golden. Drain on absorbent toweling.

Potatoes Parmigiana

Yield: 6 servings

6 medium-size potatoes	½ teaspoon black pepper
4 tablespoons butter	½ cup freshly grated
¼ cup beef broth	Parmesan cheese
1 teaspoon salt	

1. Preheat oven to 400 degrees.

2. Peel potatoes and dice very finely. Sauté in 2 tablespoons butter in a heavy skillet about 7 minutes or until barely tender.

3. Add broth, salt and pepper; turn into a greased shallow baking dish. Dot with remaining butter and sprinkle with cheese. Bake until browned, about 35 minutes.

Skillet Potatoes

Yield: 6 servings

6 Idaho potatoes

½ cup butter

Salt and black pepper

2 tablespoons finely
chopped onion

Chopped parsley

1. Peel potatoes and cut into wafer-thin slices to make 4 cups. As the potatoes are sliced, drop them into cold water with a tablespoon of vinegar. Drain potatoes and pat dry.

2. Heat half the butter in a seasoned 10-inch iron skillet and add the potatoes. Season with salt and pepper. Add onion. Cook over relatively high heat, shaking the skillet, until potatoes are limp; press down with a spatula. Reduce heat and cook until golden brown on one side. Flip potatoes like a pancake and brown on other side. The total cooking time should be about 30 minutes.

3. Heat remaining butter until almost brown. Pour it over potatoes and serve sprinkled with chopped parsley.

Potatoes in Sour Cream Sauce

Yield: 6 servings

6 medium-size potatoes	1 tablespoon snipped
2 cups boiling chicken broth	fresh dill
5 tablespoons butter	1 cup sour cream
3 tablespoons minced onion	½ teaspoon salt
1 tablespoon flour	⅛ teaspoon black pepper

1. Peel potatoes and halve. Cover with broth in a saucepan and cook, covered, until barely tender, 15 to 20 minutes. Drain and reserve ½ cup broth.

2. Melt 3 tablespoons butter in a skillet and add potatoes and onion. Sauté until potatoes are browned. Keep warm.

3. Melt remaining butter. Stir in flour. Gradually stir in reserved broth and cook over low heat, stirring constantly, until thickened. Off heat, stir in dill, sour cream, salt and pepper. Reheat but do not boil. Pour over potatoes.

Potatoes in Cream

Yield: 6 servings

6 medium-size potatoes	Salt and black pepper
7 tablespoons butter	⅛ teaspoon nutmeg
6 tablespoons flour	¾ cup bread crumbs
1 cup milk	½ cup freshly grated
1 cup light cream	Parmesan cheese

1. Preheat oven to 400 degrees.

2. Cover scrubbed potatoes with hot salted water and simmer 15 to 20 minutes, until potatoes are barely tender. Drain, peel and dice or slice into a greased 1½-quart baking dish.

3. Melt 6 tablespoons butter; blend in flour. Gradually stir in milk and cream. Bring to a boil, stirring until sauce thickens. Season with salt, pepper and nutmeg.

4. Pour sauce over the potatoes and toss lightly. Melt remaining butter; add the bread crumbs and cheese and sprinkle over top. Bake 30 minutes or until potatoes are tender.

Salads and Vegetables

Caesar Salad

Yield: 10 to 12 servings

2 cloves garlic, crushed

¾ cup olive oil

2 cups cubed stale French bread

3 quarts romaine, in bite-size pieces

½ teaspoon black pepper

½ teaspoon salt

2 eggs, cooked 1 minute in boiling water

Juice of 2 lemons

1 can anchovy fillets, diced

½ cup freshly grated Parmesan cheese

1. Add garlic to the oil and let stand several hours.

2. Heat ¼ cup garlic oil in a small skillet and sauté croutons until browned on all sides. Set aside.

3. At the table or just before serving, place romaine in salad bowl and assemble all remaining ingredients.

4. Grind pepper and sprinkle salt over romaine; add remaining ½ cup garlic oil and toss to coat greens.

284

5. Break eggs into salad, pour lemon juice over eggs and toss again. Add anchovy and cheese. Toss. Add croutons and serve immediately.

Boston Lettuce and Sour Cream Sauce

Yield: 4 to 6 servings

3 tablespoons sour cream
¼ cup heavy cream
1 tablespoon wine vinegar
1 teaspoon Dijon or
    Düsseldorf mustard
1 teaspoon finely chopped
    shallots or scallions

1 small clove garlic,
    finely minced
Salt and black pepper
    to taste
1 quart Boston lettuce
    leaves, washed, dried
    and crisped

1. Place sour cream in a mixing bowl and gradually stir in heavy cream. Stir in remaining seasonings and chill until ready to use.

2. Place greens in a salad bowl. Spoon sauce over and toss.

Spinach Salad

Yield: 8 servings

2 pounds fresh, tender spinach

1½ tablespoons soy sauce

1½ tablespoons sesame oil

1½ teaspoons sugar

1½ tablespoons vinegar

½ teaspoon monosodium glutamate

½ teaspoon salt

⅛ teaspoon minced garlic

2 tablespoons toasted sesame seeds

1. Pick over spinach to remove any tough stems and rinse under cold running water. Drop into boiling water. When the water returns to a boil, drain spinach. Let cool, then squeeze to remove excess moisture.

2. Cut spinach into 1½-inch lengths. Combine remaining ingredients except sesame seeds and pour over spinach. Toss until spinach is coated with sauce. Chill.

3. Sprinkle with sesame seeds and serve.

Provençal Salad

Yield: 6 to 8 servings

1 clove garlic, crushed
½ cup olive oil
⅓ cup lemon juice
½ teaspoon salt
  Grated rind of 2 oranges
¾ cup cured black olives,
  pitted

¾ cup celery root, in
  julienne strips
½ cup chopped parsley
3 bunches watercress,
  stems removed

1. Let garlic stand in oil, lemon juice and salt for an hour or two.

2. Place orange rind, olives, celery root and parsley in large china bowl. Cover with watercress. Chill, covered, in refrigerator.

3. At serving time, toss with oil and lemon juice (remove garlic); add salt and pepper to taste.

Malagasy
Vegetable Salad

Yield: 6 to 8 servings

1 quart lightly salted water
4 carrots, cut into julienne
    strips
1 white turnip, cut into
    julienne strips
½ small head cabbage,
    shredded
¼ pound green beans, cut
    lengthwise into strips

1 tablespoon curry powder
½ tablespoon black pepper
1 onion, finely chopped
4 tablespoons vinegar
5 tablespoons vegetable oil
Tabasco sauce

1. Bring water to a boil and add carrots, turnip, cabbage and green beans. Cook, uncovered, 5 minutes. Drain vegetables well and place in a large bowl.

2. While vegetables are still hot, sprinkle with curry and pepper. Mix well and let cool.

3. Add onion, vinegar and oil to cooled vegetables and toss. Stir in enough Tabasco to give the mixture piquancy. Chill well before serving. The vegetables will keep several days in refrigerator.

Raita

(Cucumbers with Yogurt)

Yield: 6 servings

2 cups plain yogurt
1 cucumber, peeled and
    grated
¾ teaspoon freshly ground
    cumin seeds
½ teaspoon salt, or to taste

Black pepper to taste
Cayenne pepper to taste
Chopped parsley
    (preferably Chinese
    parsley)

1. Combine yogurt, cucumber, ½ teaspoon cumin, salt and pepper in a mixing bowl. Chill.

2. Serve sprinkled with fresh pepper, cayenne, remaining cumin seeds and chopped parsley.

Watercress, Endive and Beets

Yield: 4 servings

2 medium-size beets	1 clove garlic
1 bunch watercress	2 tablespoons wine vinegar
2 heads endive	7 tablespoons olive oil
½ teaspoon salt	Black pepper to taste

1. Do not trim beets at root end; leave on 2 inches of stem. Rinse beets and place in a saucepan. Add salted water to cover. Bring to a boil and simmer until tender, 45 minutes or longer. Chill.

2. Cut off and discard tough watercress stems and rinse. Cut endive into ½-inch lengths; rinse. Shake greens to dry.

3. Pare off both ends of beets and slip off the skins. Cut beets into very thin rounds or into julienne strips.

4. Add salt to salad bowl. Rub bowl well with garlic. Add vinegar, oil and pepper and stir well with a fork. Add watercress, endive and beets. Toss and serve.

Cole Slaw with Capers

Yield: 4 to 6 servings

1 small head green
    cabbage
½ small onion
    Salt and black pepper
    to taste
2 tablespoons wine vinegar
3 tablespoons olive oil
½ teaspoon Tabasco sauce

1 teaspoon chopped fresh
    thyme, basil, tar-
    ragon, marjoram or
    other fresh herb
2 tablespoons capers
1½ cups homemade
    mayonnaise (page 244)

1. Peel off tough outer leaves and pare away core of cabbage. Slice cabbage in half and shred it finely. There should be about 4 cups.

2. Place shredded cabbage in a large bowl. Grate enough onion to make 1 or 2 teaspoons and add it to the cabbage. Add remaining ingredients, using just enough mayonnaise to bind well. Toss and chill.

Hot Herbed
Potato Salad

Yield: 4 to 6 servings

6 large, waxy potatoes

¼ cup minced parsley

2 tablespoons minced chives

3 tablespoons minced onion

½ clove garlic, minced

¼ cup peanut oil, or more to taste

Salt and black pepper to taste

1. Place unpeeled potatoes in a kettle. Add salted water to cover. Bring to a boil and simmer until potatoes are tender, 30 minutes or longer.

2. When potatoes are cool enough to handle, peel them and slice ¼ inch thick into a mixing bowl.

3. Add parsley, chives, onion and garlic. Sprinkle with oil, salt and pepper to taste. Toss lightly and serve warm.

Tomatoes with Salad Russe

Yield: 4 servings

4 medium-size ripe
   tomatoes

½ cup cooked green peas

½ cup cooked cubed carrots

½ cup cooked cubed
   potatoes

¼ cup homemade
   mayonnaise (page 244)

¼ cup sour cream

Salt and black pepper
   to taste

1 teaspoon capers

1 tablespoon finely
   chopped parsley

1 teaspoon minced onion

Lemon juice to taste

1. Pare away top of each tomato. Pare around the inside of each tomato to remove most of pulp and seeds. Sprinkle inside tomato with salt and turn upside down to drain.

2. Place peas, carrots and potatoes in bowl; add remaining ingredients. Toss until coated with mayonnaise mixture. Fill tomato shells with mixture.

293

Marinated Tomatoes

Yield: 4 servings

4 large tomatoes, skinned
  and sliced
1 cup olive oil
¼ cup wine vinegar
¼ teaspoon dry mustard
1 teaspoon salt
¼ teaspoon black pepper
1 clove garlic, finely
  chopped

1 tablespoon chopped
  fresh basil
2 sprigs fresh thyme,
  chopped
1 sprig fresh marjoram,
  chopped
1 tablespoon chopped
  scallions

1. Place tomato slices in a serving bowl.

2. Combine remaining ingredients and pour over tomatoes.
   Allow to marinate 1 hour or longer.

Zucchini and Tomato Salad

Yield: 12 servings

6 medium-size zucchini

24 slices skinned ripe
    tomatoes

Salt and black pepper

1 clove garlic, minced

¾ cup olive oil

¼ cup wine vinegar

⅓ cup chopped parsley

1. Cut off ends of each zucchini. Rinse and dry zucchini; cut on the bias into slices about ¾ inch thick. Place slices in a saucepan and add salted water to cover. Bring to a boil and simmer gently just until crisp and tender. Do not overcook. Drain immediately. Cool, then chill.

2. When ready to serve, arrange alternating slices of zucchini and tomato on a platter. Sprinkle with salt and pepper. Combine garlic, oil and vinegar and beat with fork. Pour dressing over vegetables and sprinkle with parsley.

Artichoke Fritters

Yield: 6 to 8 servings

2 packages (9 ounces each) frozen artichoke hearts

1½ cups flour

3 egg yolks

Salt and black pepper to taste

Tabasco sauce to taste

¼ teaspoon nutmeg

1¼ cups (approximately) milk

¾ teaspoon baking powder

Oil for deep-frying

1. Cook artichokes until barely tender. Drain well.

2. Place flour in a bowl and add yolks, salt, pepper, Tabasco and nutmeg. Gradually beat in 1 cup milk. Stir in baking powder; adjust consistency with milk and coat artichokes in batter.

3. Drop artichokes one at a time into deep fat heated to 360 degrees. Cook, turning, until golden brown. Drain and serve hot.

Baked Butter Beans with Pears

Yield: 18 to 24 servings

6 cups cooked dried butter, marrow or lima beans (see note)

6 ripe pears, peeled, cored and sliced

½ cup molasses

½ cup brown sugar

¼ cup finely chopped onion

1 cup chicken broth

Salt and black pepper to taste

1. Preheat oven to 180-200 degrees.

2. Combine all ingredients in a large heavy casserole. Bake, covered, 8 hours or longer, adding more broth if necessary. If there is excess moisture when ready to serve, bake 30 to 60 minutes longer uncovered to evaporate it.

Note: Drained canned beans may be substituted for fresh beans, if desired.

Green Beans with Mustard

Yield: 4 servings

1 pound fresh green beans	1 tablespoon butter
2 tablespoons salad oil	½ cup milk
1 teaspoon dry mustard	1 teaspoon white vinegar
2 egg yolks, at room	Salt and black pepper
temperature	to taste

1. Pluck off the ends of beans; cut beans into 2-inch lengths and place in a saucepan with a tight-fitting lid. Rinse beans under cold running water and drain. Add oil. Do not add salt or additional liquid. Cover tightly and cook over very low heat, tossing the pan occasionally to rearrange beans. Cook until beans are crisp-tender, about 10 minutes. Watch closely so that beans do not burn.

2. Meanwhile, combine mustard, yolks and butter in a saucepan and let stand 10 minutes.

3. Bring milk to the boiling point and add it gradually to mustard mixture, stirring rapidly. Stir over very low heat until slightly thickened. Add vinegar, salt and pepper and then add beans. Stir until beans are coated. Serve hot.

Caraway Cabbage

Yield: 4 servings

2 tablespoons butter
1 small, firm head cabbage,
    coarsely shredded
1 teaspoon salt
1 clove garlic, minced

1 teaspoon caraway seeds
1 teaspoon sugar
1½ tablespoons vinegar
½ cup sour cream

1. Heat butter in skillet. Add cabbage, salt and garlic and stir well. Cover tightly and steam 10 minutes.

2. Add caraway seeds, sugar and vinegar and mix well. Stir in sour cream and serve immediately.

299

Braised Red Cabbage

Yield: 6 servings

2 onions, sliced

¼ cup bacon fat

1 head red cabbage, finely
   shredded

2 large tart apples, peeled
   and diced

½ cup red currant jelly

1 bay leaf, crumbled

Ham bone (optional)

6 cloves

Salt and black pepper

½ cup beef broth

2 tablespoons wine vinegar

1. Preheat oven to 325 degrees.

2. In a heavy stainless steel or porcelainized iron casserole, sauté onion in bacon fat until tender.

3. Add cabbage, apples, jelly, bay leaf, ham bone, cloves, salt and pepper to taste and beef broth.

4. Cover tightly and bake 2½ hours, adding a small quantity of broth if necessary to prevent sticking. Stir occasionally.

5. Before serving, remove ham bone and stir in vinegar.

Carrot Puree

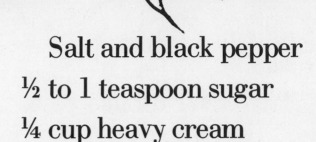

Yield: 4 to 6 servings

12 medium-size carrots,
    scraped and quartered
4 tablespoons butter

Salt and black pepper
½ to 1 teaspoon sugar
¼ cup heavy cream

1. Preheat oven to 400 degrees.

2. Place carrots in a kettle and add salted water to cover. Bring to a boil; simmer until tender. Length of time will depend on size and age of carrots. Drain.

3. Put carrots through a fine sieve or food mill. Add 3 table-spoons butter, salt and pepper to taste, sugar and cream. Pour into a buttered small baking dish. Dot with remaining butter. Bake until lightly browned on top.

Baked Cauliflower Mayonnaise

Yield: 4 to 6 servings

1 head cauliflower
  (left whole)

Salt to taste

¾ cup homemade
  mayonnaise (page 244)

2 hard-cooked eggs

1 teaspoon vinegar

1 tablespoon olive oil

½ clove garlic, finely minced

1 teaspoon Worcestershire
  sauce

¼ cup finely chopped heart
  of celery

1 tablespoon finely minced
  onion

Salt and black pepper
  to taste

Tabasco sauce to taste

1. Remove outer leaves of cauliflower; pare away part of core. Place cauliflower head (left whole) in a kettle and add approximately 1 inch of water. Sprinkle with salt, cover tightly and simmer until cauliflower is tender but still firm. Drain well and keep warm.

2. Preheat oven to 400 degrees.

3. Place mayonnaise in a mixing bowl. Put eggs through a sieve and add to the mayonnaise. Blend vinegar, oil and garlic and beat with a fork; add to mayonnaise mixture. Add Worcestershire, celery, onion, salt and pepper. Add Tabasco and, if desired, a little lemon juice.

4. Place cauliflower head in a baking dish and spoon mayonnaise mixture over it. Bake about 5 minutes and serve immediately.

Snow Peas and Water Chestnuts

Yield: 4 servings

2 tablespoons vegetable oil

1 tablespoon chopped scallion

½ clove garlic, finely chopped

¼ teaspoon salt

¼ teaspoon monosodium glutamate

¼ pound Chinese pea pods (snow peas), fresh or frozen, with tips and strings removed

¼ cup sliced water chestnuts

1 tablespoon imported soy sauce

¼ cup chicken stock

1 teaspoon cornstarch

1 teaspoon water

1. Heat oil in a heavy skillet; sauté the scallion and garlic. Sprinkle with salt and monosodium glutamate.

2. Add snow peas, water chestnuts and soy sauce and cook 1 minute, stirring. Add chicken stock; cover and cook 2 minutes.

3. Mix cornstarch with water and add to skillet, stirring. Cook, stirring, until sauce thickens, about 1 minute.

Puree of Celery Root

Yield: 4 servings

3 small celery roots or
  1 large one
2 medium-size potatoes,
  peeled

2 tablespoons butter
Salt and black pepper
  to taste
¼ cup heavy cream

1. Peel celery roots carefully and cut into quarters. Cut potatoes approximately the same size. Cover with boiling salted water and bring to a boil. Simmer 20 minutes or until vegetables are tender. Drain.

2. Put vegetables through a food mill and add butter, salt and pepper. Add heavy cream. Bring to a boil and serve hot.

Creamed Spinach

Yield: 6 to 8 servings

3 pounds fresh spinach or
    2 packages (10 ounces
    each) frozen chopped
    spinach
3 tablespoons butter
1 tablespoon grated onion
2 tablespoons flour

1 cup heavy cream
1½ teaspoons salt
¼ teaspoon black pepper
¼ teaspoon nutmeg
2 hard-cooked eggs for
    garnish

1. Wash fresh spinach; remove tough stems. Place in a pan with just water clinging to leaves. Cover and cook until wilted. Drain well and chop. There should be 3½ to 4 cups. If frozen spinach is used, cook according to package directions and drain well.

2. Melt butter in a large skillet and sauté onion 2 or 3 minutes. Sprinkle with flour. Blend in cream and bring to a boil, stirring. Add spinach, salt, pepper and nutmeg; reheat.

3. Separate yolks and whites of eggs. Sieve yolks and chop whites; use for garnish.

Endive Meunière

Yield: 4 servings

8 large endives	Juice of ½ lemon
½ cup water	1 tablespoon sugar
Salt to taste	4 tablespoons butter

1. Preheat oven to 350 degrees.

2. Lightly trim off ends of endives; place endives in a heavy 1-quart casserole. Add water, salt, lemon juice, sugar and half the butter. Cover and bring to a boil on top of stove. Bake 30 minutes, then drain well.

3. Heat remaining butter in a large skillet and add endives. Brown well on one side; turn and brown on other side. Serve immediately.

Squash Casserole

Yield: 4 servings

1 pound crookneck or
    pattypan squash
1 medium-size onion,
    chopped
1 clove garlic, chopped
2 tablespoons butter
1 canned hot green chili
    pepper, finely chopped

1 teaspoon salt
¼ teaspoon black pepper
1 egg, beaten
½ cup heavy cream
¼ cup dry white wine
⅓ cup grated sharp
    Cheddar cheese

1. Preheat oven to 350 degrees.

2. Wash but do not peel squash. Slice thinly.

3. Place in a heavy skillet with just enough water to prevent scorching and cook, covered, until barely tender. Drain well and mash squash.

4. Sauté onion and garlic in butter until tender. Add chili, salt, pepper and squash. Stir in egg, cream and wine.

5. Pour into a greased 1-quart casserole and bake 30 to 35 minutes, until set. Sprinkle cheese over top during last 10 minutes of baking.

Corn-Cheese Casserole

Yield: 4 servings

6 tablespoons butter

3 cups corn kernels, cut
   from the cob

2 tablespoons finely
   chopped onion

½ teaspoon salt

¼ teaspoon black pepper

1 cup shredded Swiss cheese

½ cup heavy cream

1. Preheat oven to 375 degrees.

2. Dot bottom of a 2-quart casserole with 3 tablespoons butter. Combine corn, onion, salt, pepper and ½ cup cheese and pour into casserole.

3. Sprinkle with remaining cheese and dot with remaining butter. Pour cream over all and bake, uncovered, until corn is tender and cheese is melted, about 20 minutes.

Baked Vegetables Country-Style

Yield: 6 to 8 servings

5 tablespoons (approximately) salad oil

1 pound spinach, coarsely chopped

4 medium-size zucchini, diced

1 cup green beans, in 1-inch pieces

1 cup chopped onion

⅛ teaspoon finely chopped garlic

2 teaspoons basil

1 teaspoon salt

½ teaspoon nutmeg

¼ teaspoon black pepper

4 eggs, lightly beaten

¼ cup freshly grated Parmesan cheese

1. Preheat oven to 350 degrees.

2. Heat 3 tablespoons oil in a skillet. Add spinach and cook until wilted, adding more oil if necessary. Place spinach in a sieve and press out liquid.

3. Add remaining oil to skillet and cook zucchini, green beans and onion over low heat, stirring occasionally, until zucchini is tender but crisp, 7 to 9 minutes.

4. Combine cooked vegetables in a bowl. Add garlic, basil, salt, nutmeg and pepper. Spoon into a buttered 2-quart casserole.

5. Pour eggs over vegetables, sprinkle with cheese and bake 40 minutes. Serve immediately.

Zucchini Smetana

Yield: 4 to 6 servings

3 or 4 zucchini
Salt and black pepper
  to taste
¾ cup sour cream
1 tablespoon snipped fresh
  dill

Tabasco sauce to taste
¼ cup freshly grated
  Parmesan cheese

1. Preheat oven to 375 degrees.

2. Trim off ends of zucchini; do not peel. Cut into ¼-inch slices and place in a buttered 1-quart baking dish. Sprinkle with salt and pepper.

3. Pour sour cream into mixing bowl and add salt, pepper, dill and Tabasco. Pour mixture over zucchini and sprinkle with cheese. Cover and bake 30 minutes. Uncover and continue baking until tender, 10 to 15 minutes longer.

Preserves, Pickles and Relishes

Spiced
Blueberry Preserve

Yield: 4 or 5 half-pint jars

1 quart blueberries (preferably wild)	¼ teaspoon ground allspice
¼ cup cider vinegar	¼ teaspoon cinnamon
2 cups sugar	⅛ teaspoon cloves

1. Wash, stem and pick over blueberries. Combine all ingredients in a heavy pan. Simmer, stirring occasionally, until blueberry skins are tender and the preserve is of desired thickness.

2. Test for set by placing a small amount of the boiling jam on a cold plate and refrigerating to cool fast. When cold, the sample should have a jelly-like set, and a finger run through the drop should leave a clean track. To make thicker, boil longer.

3. Pour into hot sterilized jars; seal with 2 thin layers of paraffin wax and cool. Cap jars and store in a cool, dark, dry place.

Strawberry-Rhubarb Jam

Yield: About 5 pints

1 quart rhubarb, in ½-inch pieces

2 quarts sugar

2 quarts strawberries

1. Place rhubarb in a large bowl and mix with sugar. Let stand overnight.

2. Bring mixture to a boil in a kettle and simmer gently 10 minutes. Add strawberries and continue simmering until mixture is thick, stirring occasionally to prevent sticking, about 10 minutes.

3. Ladle jam into hot sterilized jars; pour melted paraffin wax over surface. Cool undisturbed. Cap and store in a cool, dark, dry place.

Ginger-Peach Jam

Yield: About 10 six-ounce glasses

3½ pounds (approximately) ripe peaches

½ cup finely slivered candied ginger

1 box (1¾ ounces) powdered fruit pectin or 1 bottle liquid

5½ cups sugar

1. Peel and pit peaches. Finely chop or grind enough fruit to make 4½ cups. Place fruit and ginger in a large kettle.

2. Add pectin to kettle and stir to mix. Bring mixture to a full rolling boil. Add sugar and stir to dissolve.

3. Bring to a full rolling boil again and boil hard 1 minute, stirring constantly. Remove from heat and skim off foam. Stir and skim 5 minutes to cool slightly and prevent fruit from floating.

4. Ladle into hot sterilized jelly glasses. Cover with 2 thin layers of paraffin wax. Cool and cover. Store in a cool, dark dry place.

Plum Conserve

Yield: About 6 pints

4 pounds (approximately)
    purple plums
4 large nectarines, skinned,
    pitted and chopped
    Thin rind from 2 large
    oranges and 1 lemon,
    finely chopped

Sections from 2 peeled
    oranges, chopped
2 cups ground raisins
8 cups sugar
2 cups chopped pecans

1. Pit and chop enough plums to make 2¼ quarts. Combine all ingredients except nuts in a large kettle. Gradually bring to a boil, stirring occasionally until sugar is dissolved.

2. Cook rapidly, stirring to prevent sticking, until thick, 15 to 20 minutes. Add nuts and cook 5 minutes longer.

3. Pour immediately into hot sterilized jars and adjust caps. Cool and store in a cool, dark, dry place.

317

Spiced Pear Butter

Yield: 6 half-pint jars

5 pounds (approximately) ripe pears

¼ cup cider vinegar

¼ cup water

4 cups sugar

½ cup orange juice

¼ cup lemon juice

1½ teaspoons whole allspice, tied in a muslin bag

1. Peel and core pears. Slice enough fruit to make 12 cups. Place pears, vinegar and water in a large kettle and cook until fruit is soft. Mash down and measure. There should be 6 cups of pulp. Return to pan.

2. Add sugar, orange juice, lemon juice and spice bag. Cook and stir over medium heat until mixture is very thick, 50 to 60 minutes.

3. Discard bag and ladle into hot sterilized jars and seal at once. Cool and store in a cool, dark, dry place.

Apple Marmalade

Yield: About 8 half-pint jars

1½ cups water
5 cups sugar
2 tablespoons lemon juice
8 cups peeled, thinly sliced
    tart apples

1 orange, quartered,
    seeded and thinly
    sliced, including the
    rind

1. Heat water and sugar and stir until sugar is dissolved. Add lemon juice, apples and orange. Boil rapidly, stirring constantly, until a candy thermometer reaches 221 degrees, or until mixture thickens.

2. Remove from heat, skim and ladle into hot sterilized jars. Top with 2 thin layers of paraffin wax. Cool and cover. Store in a cool, dark, dry place.

Lemon Pickles

Yield: 2 half-pint jars

4 large lemons, thinly sliced
½ teaspoon salt
1 cup sugar
½ cup cider vinegar
1 one-inch piece cinnamon
    stick
3 whole allspice
3 cloves
2 tablespoons finely
    chopped preserved
    ginger (in syrup)
1 can or jar (7 ounces)
    pimentos, drained
    and chopped

1. Sprinkle lemon slices with salt and set aside.

2. Combine sugar and vinegar in a saucepan. Tie cinnamon, allspice and cloves in a muslin bag and add to sugar mixture. Bring to a boil; cook rapidly 5 minutes. Remove bag.

3. Add lemon slices and boil 2 minutes. Add ginger and pimentos and boil 1 minute longer.

4. Pack hot pickles in hot sterilized jars and seal. Cool and store in a cool, dark, dry place.

Tomato Marmalade

Yield: About 5 pints

3 quarts sliced skinned
    tomatoes (18 to 20)

6 cups sugar

1 teaspoon salt

2 oranges

2 lemons

2 cups water

4 cinnamon sticks (2- to
    3-inch pieces)

2 teaspoons whole cloves

1. Combine tomatoes, sugar and salt.

2. Peel oranges and lemons; slice the rind thinly. Cover with water and boil 5 minutes; drain. Slice orange and lemon pulp; remove seeds. Add pulp and rind to tomatoes.

3. Tie cinnamon sticks and cloves in a muslin bag and add to tomato mixture. Heat slowly to boiling and cook rapidly, stirring often to prevent sticking, until thickened, 45 to 60 minutes. Remove spice bag.

4. Pour marmalade into hot sterilized jars; seal. Cool and store in a cool, dark, dry place.

Pickled Cantaloupe

Yield: 7 pints

4 medium-size cantaloupes (9 to 10 pounds)

3 quarts plus 1 cup water

2 teaspoons alum (available in drugstores)

4 cups sugar

2 cups white vinegar

4 three-inch cinnamon sticks

1 tablespoon whole cloves

1 tablespoon whole allspice

1. Halve melons lengthwise and remove seeds and rind. Cut each half into quarters and then each quarter into ¼-inch pieces.

2. Combine 3 quarts of water and alum and pour over melon; cover and let stand overnight. Drain and rinse melon.

3. In a deep kettle, combine sugar, vinegar and remaining water. Tie spices in a muslin bag and add to kettle; boil 5 minutes, stirring until sugar is dissolved. Add melon and simmer uncovered 20 minutes, stirring occasionally.

4. Remove the spice bag. Pack melon into hot sterilized jars. Pour in boiling syrup to within ⅛ inch of top.

5. Make sure that melon is covered in jars. Seal jars at once. Cool and store in a cool, dark, dry place.

Pickled Garden Carrots

Yield: 4 to 6 servings

1 pound freshly picked
    small carrots

2 cups water

½ cup wine vinegar

1 teaspoon salt

1 teaspoon sugar

1 teaspoon mustard seeds

1 teaspoon peppercorns

1 bay leaf

1. Trim carrots at both ends. Scrub carrots well.

2. Combine carrots with remaining ingredients and cook until tender but still crisp. Cooking time will depend on the size of the carrots. Cool the carrots in the liquid, then drain and chill. They will keep for a week if refrigerated.

Kim Chee
(Korean Pickled Cabbage)

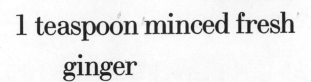

Yield: About 1 quart

2 pounds celery cabbage (Chinese cabbage)	1 teaspoon minced fresh ginger
½ cup coarse salt	1 tablespoon sugar
1½ tablespoons crushed red pepper flakes	2 scallions, finely chopped
1 clove garlic, finely minced	

1. Rinse cabbage in cold water and drain. Cut into 1½-inch pieces. Sprinkle with salt, add 1 quart water and let stand overnight.

2. Rinse cabbage in cold water and drain. Using a wooden spoon, blend remaining ingredients and stir into cabbage pieces. Pack into jars and cover. Place jars in plastic bags to prevent odors from spreading to other foods. Refrigerate and let stand 4 to 5 days to cure.

Winter Chutney

Yield: About 6 pints

3 tart apples, diced

1 cup thinly sliced sweet
  onion rings

2 cloves garlic

1 cup white seedless raisins

2 lemons, thinly sliced

2 cups pineapple chunks,
  drained

2 cups white vinegar

3 cups sugar

1 tablespoon finely chopped
  fresh ginger or 1
  teaspoon powdered

¼ teaspoon cayenne pepper

2 cans or jars (7 ounces
  each) pimentos, drained

1. Combine all ingredients except pimentos in a large kettle; bring to a boil quickly. Reduce heat and simmer slowly 1 hour or until very thick, stirring occasionally.

2. Coarsely chop pimentos and stir into mixture. Cook 20 minutes longer, stirring frequently.

3. Spoon hot relish into hot sterilized jars and seal. Cool and store in a cool, dark, dry place.

Fresh Plum Chutney

Yield: 8 half-pint jars

¾ cup cider vinegar

¾ cup water

1 cup sugar

½ teaspoon salt

3 cinnamon sticks

1 dried ginger root

½ teaspoon whole allspice

½ teaspoon whole cloves

3 pounds Italian prune plums, pitted and quartered (8 to 9 cups)

1½ cups diced peeled apples

1 cup raisins

⅓ cup finely chopped onion

1. Mix vinegar, water, sugar, salt and cinnamon in a large kettle. Tie ginger root, allspice and cloves in a muslin bag and add to kettle. Bring to a boil and boil 2 minutes.

2. Add plums, apples, raisins and onion. Cook over medium heat, stirring frequently, until the mixture thickens, 30 to 40 minutes. Discard muslin bag.

3. Pour into hot sterilized jars. Seal at once. Cool and store in a cool, dark, dry place at least 6 weeks before serving.

Breads

C.D.Q. Bread
(Can-Do-Quick)

Yield: 1 large loaf

2 packages active dry
    yeast
¾ cup lukewarm water
1¼ cups buttermilk
4½ to 5 cups flour
¼ cup shortening

2 tablespoons sugar
2 teaspoons baking
    powder
2 teaspoons salt
Soft butter

1. Dissolve yeast in lukewarm water in large mixer bowl.

2. Add buttermilk, 2½ cups flour, shortening, sugar, baking powder and salt. Blend 30 seconds at low speed. Beat 2 minutes at medium speed.

3. Stir in remaining flour to give a soft and slightly sticky dough. Knead on a floured board until satiny smooth, non-sticky and very pliable, 3 to 5 minutes.

4. Roll dough into an 18-by-9-inch rectangle. Roll up from short side jelly-roll fashion; press ends to seal and fold under. Place seam side down in greased 9-by-5-by-3-inch loaf pan (preferably metal).

5. Brush top of loaf with soft butter, cover and let rise in warm place until doubled in bulk, about 1 hour. Dough will rise at least 2 inches above pan in center.

6. Preheat oven to 425 degrees.

7. Bake 30 to 35 minutes or until loaf is golden and sounds hollow when tapped on bottom. Brush top with butter and cool on rack.

Whole Wheat Bread

Yield: 2 loaves

1 package active dry yeast	1 tablespoon sugar
2 cups lukewarm water	3 cups whole wheat flour
1 tablespoon salt	3 cups (approximately) flour

1. Dissolve yeast in lukewarm water and add salt and sugar, stirring thoroughly.

2. Add flour, alternating 1 cup of whole wheat flour and 1 cup of regular, beating it in with wooden spoon. Or use dough hook on an electric mixer at low speed. Add enough flour to make a fairly stiff dough.

3. When dough is thoroughly mixed, shape it into a ball; place in a clean greased bowl and grease the top of dough with oil. Cover with a towel and let rise in a warm place until doubled in bulk.

330

4. Turn dough onto a lightly floured board and shape into 2 long French-style loaves or round Italian-style loaves. Arrange on baking sheet heavily sprinkled with corn-meal and allow to rise 5 minutes.

5. Slash tops of loaves in 2 or 3 places with knife or scissors. Brush loaves with water and place in a cold oven. Set oven control at 400 degrees and turn oven on. Place a pan of boiling water on bottom of oven. Bake loaves until crusty and done, 40 to 45 minutes.

Rye Bread

Yield: 2 loaves

1 package active dry yeast

¼ cup lukewarm water

2 cups scalded milk

2 tablespoons butter

2 teaspoons salt

2 tablespoons sugar

2 cups rye flour

4 cups (approximately) flour

1 tablespoon caraway seeds

1 egg white

1 tablespoon water

1. Dissolve yeast in lukewarm water.

2. Pour milk into a large mixing bowl. Add butter, salt and sugar and stir to melt and dissolve. Cool to lukewarm.

3. Add yeast to milk. Stir in rye flour and enough regular flour to make a soft but not sticky dough. Add seeds.

4. Knead dough on a lightly floured board until smooth, about 10 minutes. Form into a ball and place in clean greased bowl. Grease top of dough with oil, cover and let rise in a warm place until doubled in bulk, about 1 hour.

5. Punch down dough. Knead briefly. Divide in half.

6. Form into 2 loaves. Fit into 2 greased 9-by-3-inch loaf pans or place on a greased, cornmeal-sprinkled baking sheet.

7. Cover and let rise until doubled in bulk, about 45 minutes.

8. Preheat oven to 375 degrees (350 degrees if using glass loaf pans). Brush tops of risen loaves with egg white beaten with water. Bake 45 minutes or until loaf sounds hollow when tapped on bottom.

Note: For darker bread, dough can be made with 3 cups rye flour and 3 cups regular flour, with or without replacing ½ cup milk with ½ cup molasses. If molasses is used, omit sugar and increase salt to 3 teaspoons.

Pumpernickel Bread

Yield: 3 loaves

2 cups cold mashed
  potatoes
¾ cup yellow cornmeal
3½ cups lukewarm water
2 squares unsweetened
  chocolate, melted
¼ cup molasses
2 tablespoons salt

1 tablespoon butter
2 teaspoons caraway seeds
2 packages active dry
  yeast
3 cups unsifted rye flour
1 cup whole bran cereal
8 cups (approximately)
  unsifted flour

1. In a large bowl, combine potatoes, cornmeal, 3 cups luke-warm water, chocolate, molasses, salt, butter and cara-way seeds.

2. Place remaining lukewarm water in a very large bowl. Sprinkle on yeast and stir to dissolve. Stir in cornmeal mixture, rye flour and bran cereal. Beat until well mixed.

3. Stir in 3 cups regular flour to make a soft dough.

4. Turn onto a floured board and knead in enough additional flour to make a smooth and elastic dough, about 10 minutes. Place dough in a greased bowl and turn to grease the top; cover and let rise in a warm place until doubled in bulk, about 1 hour.

5. Punch down dough; let rise again 30 minutes.

6. Punch down; turn onto a lightly floured board. Divide dough into 3 equal parts, shape into loaves and place in greased 9-by-5-by-3-inch loaf pans. Cover and let rise until doubled in bulk, about 45 minutes.

7. Preheat oven to 350 degrees.

8. Bake loaves about 1 hour or until done.

Pissaladière Provençale

Yield: 8 servings

2 teaspoons chopped fresh
thyme leaves or 1 tea-
spoon dried
1 bay leaf, crumbled
½ cup olive oil
6 large onions, sliced
¼ cup water

5 large anchovy fillets
1 pound bread dough,
homemade or from
bakery (see note)
⅓ to ½ cup pitted Greek or
Italian black olives

1. Add thyme and bay leaf to half the oil in a heavy skillet or saucepan. Cook briefly.

2. Add onions and cook over very low heat for 15 minutes, stirring occasionally. At no time should onions brown; they should be kept as white as possible.

3. Add water and cover. Cook over low heat 1 hour, adding more water if necessary to prevent scorching.

4. Add anchovies and cook 10 minutes longer, uncovered.

5. Remove from heat; transfer to a bowl. Pour remaining oil over surface and let stand in refrigerator overnight.

6. Preheat oven to 350 degrees.

7. Grease a 12- or 14-inch round pizza pan or a large cooky sheet. Roll or stretch bread dough to fit pan, forming a raised edge.

8. Pour in onion mixture and dot with olives. Bake 30 minutes or until done. Serve cold.

Note: Some bread bakers will sell dough. One such is Zito's, 259 Bleecker Street, in New York, where the dough costs 35 cents a pound and one day's notice is required.

Gugelhupf

Yield: 10 to 12 servings

1 package active dry yeast	Grated rind of 1 lemon
¼ cup lukewarm water	¾ cup milk, scalded and
¾ cup soft butter	cooled to lukewarm
½ cup sugar	½ cup raisins
6 egg yolks	⅓ cup slivered blanched
2½ cups flour	almonds
½ teaspoon salt	Confectioners' sugar

1. Dissolve yeast in lukewarm water.

2. Beat butter and sugar together until light and fluffy. Beat in egg yolks, one at a time.

3. Beat in yeast mixture. Combine flour, salt and lemon rind and beat slowly into batter alternately with the milk.

4. Beat at low speed on an electric mixer or by hand for about 3 minutes, until batter is smooth and elastic.

338

5. Stir in raisins and nuts and pour into a well-greased 9-inch (2-quart) gugelhupf pan. Batter will half fill pan.

6. Cover with clear plastic wrap and a moist towel and set in warm place, away from drafts, to rise until batter almost fills pan, 2½ to 4 hours.

7. Preheat oven to 400 degrees.

8. Bake cake 10 minutes. Reduce heat to 350 degrees and bake 25 minutes longer or until done. Cool in pan at least 10 minutes before turning onto rack to cool.

9. Cake should be tightly wrapped in aluminum foil and stored at least 24 hours before serving. Sprinkle with confectioners' sugar.

Babka

1 package active dry yeast	3 eggs
¼ cup lukewarm milk	2½ cups flour
¼ cup lukewarm water	¼ teaspoon salt
¼ cup sugar	¼ cup candied fruits
¼ cup butter	¼ cup raisins

1. Dissolve yeast in milk and water. Add ½ teaspoon sugar, stir and set aside in a warm place.

2. Combine butter, remaining sugar, eggs, flour and salt in a large bowl. When yeast mixture bubbles, beat into flour mixture until smooth. Clean sides of the bowl. Cover with a damp cloth and let rise in a warm place until doubled in bulk, about 1 hour.

3. Stir in fruits and raisins and turn onto a lightly floured board. Knead 1 to 2 minutes.

4. Put dough in a greased 2-quart mold or gugelhupf pan. Cover; let rise until doubled in bulk, about 45 minutes.

5. Preheat oven to 375 degrees.

6. Bake 35 minutes or until golden brown and done. Remove from pan immediately and brush with Rum Glaze (below).

Rum Glaze: Mix ½ cup sugar with 2 tablespoons water and 2 tablespoons light rum in small saucepan. Bring to a boil and boil briskly 1 minute.

Basic Sweet Dough

1¼ cups milk, scalded   ½ cup lukewarm water
 ½ cup butter   2 eggs
 2 teaspoons salt   6½ cups (approximately)
 ⅓ cup sugar   flour
 2 packages active dry
   yeast

1. Combine milk, butter, salt and sugar in a bowl. Cool to lukewarm.

2. Dissolve yeast in lukewarm water. Add yeast, eggs and half the flour to bowl.

3. Beat with a wooden spoon until smooth, or use dough hook of electric mixer to beat 1 minute at slow speed and 3 minutes at medium speed.

4. Mix in remaining flour by stirring and then kneading on a board to make a soft, smooth dough, or add to bowl and beat with dough hook 2 minutes at medium speed.

5. Place dough in a greased bowl, cover and let rise in a warm place until doubled in bulk. Punch down, turn onto a lightly floured board; divide into 3 parts. Use 2 parts for the Pecan Raisin Whirls (page 344) and 1 part for the Kolache (below).

Kolache
Yield: 12 rolls

⅓ basic sweet dough (left)
6 tablespoons raspberry
   preserves or orange
   marmalade

3 tablespoons melted butter
Confectioners' sugar

1. Divide dough into 12 pieces. Shape each into a ball and place 2 inches apart on a greased baking sheet. With 2 fingers, make a depression in center; fill with preserves. Cover and let rise in a warm place until doubled.

2. Preheat oven to 350 degrees.

3. Bake rolls 18 to 20 minutes. Brush with butter and sprinkle with sugar.

343

Pecan Raisin Whirls

Yield: 2 dozen rolls

⅔ cup melted butter

1½ cups brown sugar

4 tablespoons maple
syrup

2 cups pecan halves

1 cup chopped pecans

1 cup raisins

⅔ basic sweet dough
(page 342)

1. Combine 6 tablespoons butter with ⅔ cup sugar and the syrup. Arrange pecan halves in 2 dozen greased large muffin pans. Spoon butter mixture over them.

2. Roll half the dough into a 12-inch square on a lightly floured board. Spread with half the remaining butter and sugar. Sprinkle with half the chopped nuts and raisins. Roll jelly-roll fashion and cut into 12 slices.

3. Arrange slices, cut side up, in muffin pans. Repeat with other half of dough.

4. Place muffin pans, covered, in a warm place until rolls double in bulk.

5. Preheat oven to 350 degrees.

6. Bake about 20 minutes. Immediately turn pan upside down onto a tray. Wait 1 minute before removing pans.

Boone Tavern
Spoon Bread

Yield: 6 to 8 servings

1¼ cups white cornmeal

3 cups milk, rapidly boiling

3 eggs, well beaten

1 teaspoon salt

1¾ teaspoons baking powder

2 tablespoons melted butter

1. Stir meal into milk and cook, stirring constantly to prevent scorching. Remove from heat and allow to cool. It will be very stiff.

2. Preheat oven to 375 degrees.

3. Add remaining ingredients to cold meal mixture and beat at high speed with an electric mixer for 15 minutes, until smooth. Pour into a greased 1½-quart casserole and bake 30 minutes or until done. Serve directly from the casserole by spoonfuls.

Note: Spoon bread is served with butter and eaten with a fork.

Apple Muffins

Yield: About 20 two-inch muffins

1¼ cups bran

⅔ cup milk

2 eggs

1 cup sugar

¼ cup melted shortening
    or vegetable oil

1 cup flour

2½ teaspoons baking powder

½ teaspoon salt

¾ teaspoon cinnamon

¼ teaspoon cloves

1 cup finely chopped
    apples

1 cup raisins

1. Preheat oven to 400 degrees.

2. Combine bran, milk, eggs, sugar and shortening or oil in a bowl. Sift together flour, baking powder, salt, cinnamon and cloves and add to the batter.

3. Stir in apples and raisins and spoon into well-greased or paper-lined muffin tins. Bake 25 minutes or until done. Serve hot.

Note: Serve the muffins with whipped cream for dessert.

Lemon Muffins

Yield: About 10 muffins

2 lemons

1 cup flour

1 teaspoon baking powder

¼ teaspoon salt

½ cup butter

½ cup plus 2 tablespoons sugar

2 eggs, separated

¼ teaspoon cinnamon

1. Preheat oven to 375 degrees.

2. Grate rind off both lemons (there should be about 1 tablespoonful). Squeeze 3 tablespoons juice and set aside.

3. Sift together flour, baking powder and salt.

4. Cream butter with ½ cup sugar until light and fluffy. Beat in egg yolks one at a time. Add flour mixture alternately with lemon juice. Do not overmix.

5. Beat whites until stiff but not dry, and fold with grated rind into batter. Fill lightly greased muffin tins ¾ full.

6. Combine remaining sugar and cinnamon and sprinkle over muffins. Bake 25 minutes or until done. Serve hot.

Corn Bread

Yield: 6 servings

2 tablespoons butter	¾ cup yellow cornmeal
¼ cup sugar	4 teaspoons baking powder
1 egg	¼ teaspoon salt
1 cup flour	1 cup milk

1. Preheat oven to 350 degrees.

2. Cream butter and sugar until light and smooth. Add egg and beat well.

3. Sift dry ingredients together twice and add to creamed mixture alternately with milk, mixing well after each addition.

4. Pour batter into a greased 8-inch square pan and bake 35 to 40 minutes. Cut into squares.

Maple Fruit and Nut Bread

Yield: 2 loaves

½ cup diced dried apricots	1½ teaspoons salt
½ cup chopped dates	1 cup brown sugar
1 cup chopped walnuts	1 egg, lightly beaten
3 cups flour	1 cup milk
3 teaspoons baking powder	½ cup maple syrup
¼ teaspoon baking soda	

1. Cover apricots with boiling water. Let stand 15 minutes. Drain and chop.

2. Mix apricots, dates and nuts. Sift together flour, baking powder, soda and salt. Add brown sugar and date mixture and mix. Combine egg and milk, add syrup and stir into dry ingredients. Pour into 2 well-greased 8½-by-4½-inch loaf pans. Let stand 15 to 20 minutes before baking.

3. Preheat oven to 350 degrees.

4. Bake 50 minutes or until done. Cool on a rack.

Cakes and Cookies

Walnut Cake

Yield: 8 servings

½ cup soft butter
1 cup sugar
6 eggs, separated
1 package (6 ounces) zwieback, rolled into fine crumbs
½ cup flour
1 teaspoon baking powder
¼ teaspoon salt

½ cup orange juice
2 teaspoons grated orange rind
1½ cups very finely ground walnuts
¾ cup sieved apricot preserves
Confectioners' sugar

1. Grease and line bottoms of two 9-inch layer pans with wax paper.

2. Preheat oven to 325 degrees.

3. Cream butter and sugar until light and fluffy. Add yolks, one at a time, beating well after each addition.

4. Combine zwieback crumbs, flour, baking powder and salt. Add to butter-sugar mixture alternately with the orange juice.

5. Stir in rind and nuts. Beat whites until stiff but not dry; fold into batter.

6. Pour batter into prepared pans; bake 35 to 40 minutes. Cool layers in pans 15 minutes. Turn onto rack to complete cooling.

7. Sandwich cooled layers together with preserves. Sprinkle top with confectioners' sugar.

Lane Cake

Yield: 8 to 10 servings

Layers:

1 cup soft butter

2 cups sugar

1 teaspoon vanilla

3¼ cups flour

3½ teaspoons baking powder

¼ teaspoon salt

1 cup milk

8 egg whites

Filling:

8 egg yolks

1¼ cups sugar

Grated rind of 1 orange

⅓ cup bourbon

½ teaspoon mace

1¼ cups pecans, chopped

¼ teaspoon salt

1 cup shredded coconut

1 cup raisins

1 cup glacé cherries, quartered

1. Preheat oven to 375 degrees.

2. Beat butter and sugar together until light and creamy. Beat in vanilla.

354

3. Sift together flour, baking powder and salt twice. Stir flour mixture into batter alternately with milk.

4. Beat egg whites until stiff but not dry. Stir ¼ of whites into batter. Fold in remaining whites until just mixed.

5. Spoon into 3 greased and floured 9-inch layer pans and bake 20 to 25 minutes. Cool in pans for 10 minutes; turn onto cake racks.

6. To prepare filling, mix together yolks, sugar and orange rind in a heavy pan or in top of a double boiler.

7. Cook over medium heat, stirring constantly, until sugar dissolves and mixture thickens enough to coat back of spoon. Do not allow to boil or eggs will scramble.

8. Remove from heat and stir in remaining ingredients. Cool before using to fill and top the cake layers.

Easy Cake

Yield: 2 layers, 1 sheet cake or 3 dozen cupcakes

Cake:

½ cup soft shortening

2½ cups cake flour

3 teaspoons baking powder

1 teaspoon salt

1½ cups sugar

1 cup milk

1 teaspoon vanilla

2 eggs

Chocolate Frosting:

⅓ cup sugar

¼ cup light corn syrup

2 squares unsweetened chocolate

3 tablespoons butter

1 egg, lightly beaten

¼ teaspoon vanilla

1⅓ cups flaked coconut

1. Preheat oven to 350 degrees for layers and sheet cake, 375 degrees for cupcakes.

2. Stir shortening in large mixing bowl to soften. Sift together flour, baking powder, salt and sugar; add to shortening. Add ¾ cup milk and vanilla. Mix on low speed until moistened. Beat 2 minutes on medium speed or 300 strokes by hand.

356

3. Add eggs and remaining milk, and beat 1 minute longer or 150 strokes by hand.

4. Pour batter into two 9-inch layer pans lined on bottom with wax paper or into a 13-by-9-by-2-inch baking pan lined on bottom with paper, or spoon into 3 dozen medium-size cupcake liners set in muffin tins, filling each half full.

5. Bake layers 25 to 30 minutes, sheet 40 to 45 minutes, cupcakes 20 to 25 minutes. Cool in pans 10 minutes, then turn onto racks to cool before frosting.

6. To prepare frosting, combine sugar and corn syrup in a small saucepan. Quickly bring to a boil over high heat, stirring. Reduce heat and continue cooking and stirring until sugar is dissolved, about 1 minute. Remove from heat.

7. Add chocolate and butter; stir until melted. Gradually add to egg, blending well. Pour back into pan and cook 1 minute longer, stirring constantly.

8. Remove from heat; add vanilla and coconut. Use to frost cooled cakes or cupcakes.

Banana-Sour Cream Coffeecake

Yield: 8 to 10 servings

Layers:
 ½ cup soft butter
 1½ cups sugar
  3 eggs
 2½ cups cake flour
  ¾ teaspoon baking powder
  ¾ teaspoon baking soda
 ½ teaspoon salt
 1¼ cups mashed bananas
     (about 3)
 ½ cup sour cream

Filling:
 ¼ cup soft butter
  1 cup confectioners'
     sugar
 ¼ cup mashed banana
 ¼ teaspoon vanilla
   Whipped cream
  6 banana slices, dipped
     in lemon juice

1. Preheat oven to 350 degrees.

2. Cream butter and sugar well. Add eggs, one at a time, beating after each addition.

358

3. Sift together flour, baking powder, soda and salt; add gradually to egg mixture. Fold in mashed bananas and sour cream. Mix well.

4. Pour batter into 2 greased and floured 8- or 9-by-2-inch layer pans. Bake 40 to 45 minutes. Cool in pans 10 minutes; turn onto rack to cool.

5. For filling, cream butter and sugar together. Add banana and vanilla and beat well. Spread between cake layers. Frost top and sides of cake with whipped cream and decorate top with banana slices. Refrigerate until ready to serve.

Almond Cream Cake

Yield: 6 servings

Cake:

  1 cup heavy cream

  2 eggs

  ¾ teaspoon almond extract

  1½ cups flour

  1 cup sugar

  2 teaspoons baking powder

  ⅛ teaspoon salt

Topping:

  2 tablespoons butter

  ⅓ cup sugar

  ¼ cup blanched slivered almonds

  1 tablespoon heavy cream

  1 tablespoon flour

1. Preheat oven to 350 degrees.

2. Whip cream until it holds stiff peaks. Beat in eggs, one at a time, very well. Add extract.

3. Sift together flour, sugar, baking powder and salt; stir into batter.

4. Pour into a greased and floured 8-inch springform pan.

5. Bake 35 minutes or until lightly browned and a toothpick inserted in center comes out clean.

6. Combine topping ingredients in a small pan and stir over low heat until blended. Pour over the cake and bake 10 minutes longer. Cool on rack. The cake shrinks as it cools. Remove side of pan after 20 minutes' cooling.

Nutmeg Cake

Yield: 8 servings

2 cups brown sugar	1 teaspoon nutmeg
2 cups flour	1 cup sour cream
½ cup soft butter	1 teaspoon baking soda
1 egg	½ cup chopped nuts

1. Preheat oven to 350 degrees.

2. With fingers blend brown sugar, flour and butter to make crumbs. Spread half the crumbs in a greased 9-inch square pan 1½ inches deep or 7-inch springform pan, 3 inches deep.

3. Stir egg, nutmeg and sour cream mixed with soda into remaining crumbs. Pour batter over crumbs in pan and sprinkle with chopped nuts. Bake square cake 35 to 40 minutes; springform pan, 1½ hours at 325 degrees.

Orange Cake

Yield: 10 servings

1 cup soft butter
1½ cups sugar
3 eggs, separated
2 cups flour
1 teaspoon baking powder
1 teaspoon baking soda

1 cup sour cream
Grated rind of 1 orange
½ cup chopped walnuts
¼ cup orange juice
⅓ cup Grand Marnier
Slivered almonds

1. Preheat oven to 350 degrees.

2. Cream butter and 1 cup sugar. Beat in yolks. Sift together flour, baking powder and soda; stir into butter mixture alternately with sour cream. Stir in rind and nuts.

3. Beat egg whites until stiff but not dry and fold into batter. Pour batter into a greased 9-inch tube pan. Bake 50 minutes or until cake tests done.

4. Mix remaining sugar, juice and liqueur. Spoon over hot cake. Decorate with slivered almonds. Cool cake in pan.

363

Yogurt Coffeecake

Yield: 12 servings

Cake:
- ½ cup soft butter
- 2 cups sugar
- 2 eggs
- 2½ cups flour
- 1 teaspoon baking soda
- ⅛ teaspoon salt
- 1 cup plain yogurt
- ½ cup finely chopped mixed candied fruit

Syrup:
- 1 cup water
- 1 cup sugar
- ¼ cup orange juice
- ¼ cup ginger-flavored brandy or dark rum

1. Preheat oven to 350 degrees.

2. Cream butter and sugar until light and fluffy. Beat in eggs, one at a time, very well.

3. Sift together flour, soda and salt and add to batter alternately with yogurt. Stir in fruit.

4. Spoon batter into a well-greased bundt pan or a 9-inch tube pan. Bake about 1 hour or until cake is done.

5. Meanwhile, prepare syrup. Combine water and sugar in a small pan. Heat, stirring, until sugar is dissolved and then boil rapidly 5 minutes. Add orange juice and brandy.

6. Remove cake onto rack over a piece of wax paper. While still hot, spoon hot syrup over cake.

Spicy Butterscotch Chiffon Cake

Yield: 12 servings

2¼ cups cake flour

3 teaspoons baking powder

1 teaspoon salt

½ teaspoon allspice

½ teaspoon cinnamon

½ teaspoon cloves

½ teaspoon nutmeg

2⅔ cups granulated
brown sugar

½ cup salad oil

5 egg yolks

¾ cup water

2 teaspoons vanilla

1 cup egg whites (8 to 10),
at room temperature

½ teaspoon cream of tartar

1. Preheat oven to 325 degrees.

2. Sift together flour, baking powder, salt and spices. Stir in sugar and make a well in the center. Add oil, yolks, water and vanilla. Beat thoroughly until sugar is dissolved and batter is smooth. This step is important when granulated brown sugar is used.

3. Beat egg whites and cream of tartar until stiff but not dry. Using a rubber spatula, fold batter into egg whites gently. Do not overmix.

4. Turn mixture into an ungreased 10-inch tube pan. Bake on low shelf until cake springs back when touched lightly, 80 to 85 minutes. Invert over a funnel to cool.

5. To remove from pan, insert a sharp, thin-bladed knife around side of pan, tap pan sharply and cake will come free.

Daffodil Cake

Yield: 10 to 12 servings

1¼ cups sugar

2¼ cups flour

3 teaspoons baking powder

1 teaspoon salt

½ cup vegetable oil

5 egg yolks

¾ cup fresh orange juice

1 cup egg whites (about 6)

½ teaspoon cream of tartar

1 tablespoon grated
   orange rind

1. Preheat oven to 325 degrees.

2. Sift sugar, flour, baking powder and salt into bowl. Make a well in center. Pour oil, egg yolks and juice into well. Blend mixture to moisten and then beat 2 minutes.

3. Beat egg whites until frothy. Add cream of tartar and beat until soft peaks form. Pour egg yolk mixture over beaten whites; add rind and fold in until just blended.

4. Spoon mixture into an ungreased 10-inch tube pan and bake until a cake tester comes out clean, about 1 hour.

368

5. Invert pan while cake cools. Cool before removing from pan. If desired, frost with Orange Frosting (below).

Orange Frosting

Yield: About 3 cups

½ cup sugar
1 cup corn syrup
1 cup orange marmalade
⅓ cup water

3 egg whites, at room temperature
2 tablespoons grated orange rind

1. Combine sugar, corn syrup, marmalade and water in a saucepan. Bring to a boil, stirring until sugar dissolves. Boil until it spins a thread and reaches 236 degrees.

2. Just before end point of boiling is reached, beat egg whites until soft peaks form. Add syrup in a thin stream while beating vigorously until frosting stands in stiff peaks.

3. Fold in orange rind and use to frost Daffodil Cake. The cake may be cut into 2 or 3 layers and frosted between layers.

Mrs. Davis' Apple Cake

Yield: 6 servings

Cake:

2 cups flour

½ cup sugar

1 tablespoon baking powder

Dash of salt

½ cup soft butter

1 egg

Filling:

5 tart apples

½ cup sugar

Juice of ½ lemon

¼ cup raisins

½ teaspoon cinnamon

1. Sift flour, sugar, baking powder and salt into a mixing bowl. Add butter and egg. Knead until dough is firm and shapes easily into a ball. Wrap in wax paper; refrigerate 1 hour.

2. Meanwhile, peel apples and cut into small pieces. Add sugar, lemon juice, raisins and cinnamon and let mixture steep until dough is ready.

3. Preheat oven to 350 degrees.

4. Butter a 9-inch springform pan. Divide the dough into thirds. Roll out ⅓ of dough and line bottom of form. Roll out another ⅓ of dough and line inside of form halfway to top, pressing along bottom rim to seal bottom and sides.

5. Drain fruit mixture and pour into pastry-lined pan. Roll out remaining dough and use a pastry cutter to make long strips. Place strips crisscross on top of filling. Bake until golden brown, 45 to 55 minutes.

Orange-Oatmeal Cake

Yield: 12 servings

Cake:

1½ cups orange juice

1 cup quick-cooking rolled oats

½ cup soft butter

1 cup sugar

½ cup brown sugar

2 eggs

1 teaspoon vanilla

1¾ cups flour

1 teaspoon baking powder

1 teaspoon baking soda

½ teaspoon salt

¼ teaspoon cinnamon

1 tablespoon grated orange rind

½ cup chopped walnuts

Orange Topping:

½ cup brown sugar

¼ cup butter

1 tablespoon grated orange rind

1 tablespoon orange juice

1 cup flaked coconut

½ cup chopped walnuts

1. Preheat oven to 350 degrees.

2. Bring orange juice to a boil and pour over oats; set aside.

3. Cream butter and sugars until light. Beat in eggs and vanilla. Beat well.

4. Sift together flour, baking powder, soda, salt and cinnamon and add to batter alternately with oats.

5. Stir in rind and nuts and pour into a greased 13-by-9-by-2-inch pan. Bake 40 minutes.

6. For topping, combine sugar, butter, rind and juice in a small pan. Bring to a boil and cook 1 minute, stirring constantly. Add remaining ingredients and spread on top of cooled cake. Place cake under broiler for about 1 minute or until topping is bubbly. Serve warm or cold.

Buttermilk Gingerbread

Yield: 9 to 12 servings

½ cup shortening	1 teaspoon salt
½ cup sugar	1½ teaspoons baking soda
1 cup unsulphured	1 teaspoon ginger
molasses	2 teaspoons cinnamon
2 eggs	½ teaspoon cloves
2½ cups flour	1 cup buttermilk

1. Preheat oven to 350 degrees. Grease a 9-inch square pan and line with wax paper.

2. Cream shortening; add sugar and cream mixture until fluffy. Blend in molasses. Beat in eggs, one at a time.

3. Sift together flour, salt, baking soda and spices. Add to creamed mixture alternately with buttermilk. Turn into prepared pan and bake 40 minutes.

Florentines

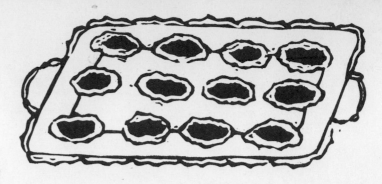

Yield: About 2 dozen cookies

½ cup heavy cream

3 tablespoons butter

½ cup sugar

1¼ cups finely chopped
   blanched almonds

⅓ cup flour

¾ cup finely chopped
   candied orange peel

1. Preheat oven to 350 degrees.

2. In a saucepan, combine the cream, butter and sugar and bring to a boil. Remove from heat and stir in remaining ingredients.

3. Drop batter by spoonfuls, 3 inches apart, onto a greased baking sheet. Bake 10 minutes.

4. Cool 5 minutes and remove with a spatula to a rack. Tops may be spread with melted chocolate.

Pirkko's Spoon Cookies

Yield: About 2½ dozen cookies

14 tablespoons unsalted
    butter
½ and ⅓ cups confectioners'
    sugar
1 teaspoon vanilla
2¼ cups flour

1½ teaspoons baking
    powder
Apple marmalade
    or other preserve
Confectioners' sugar

1. Preheat oven to 375 degrees.

2. Place butter in heavy pan and heat slowly until it browns slightly. Shake gently during last part of heating to prevent burning sediment. Remove from heat when butter has a deep golden color. Pour into heatproof bowl.

3. Mix with the 2 quantities of confectioners' sugar. Stir in vanilla and allow mixture to cool.

4. Sift together flour and baking powder; stir into batter.

5. Fill a teaspoon with batter; level off with a spatula. Slide, flat side down, onto an ungreased baking sheet. Bake 10 minutes or until lightly browned.

6. Cool on a rack. When cookies are cool, sandwich two together with marmalade or preserves in middle and dust with confectioners' sugar.

Vivian's Chocolate Lace

Yield: About 30 cookies

½ cup butter
1 tablespoon flour
½ cup sugar
1 tablespoon heavy cream
1 tablespoon milk
¾ cup ground almonds (½ cup
    blanched shelled almonds,
    ground in a blender)

4 ounces semisweet
    chocolate bits
½ to 1 ounce cocoa butter
    (available in
    drugstores)

1. Preheat oven to 350 degrees.

2. Place butter, flour, sugar, cream and milk in a small pan and heat slowly until butter is melted. Stir in almonds.

3. Grease and flour large baking sheet. Spoon 5 well-spaced teaspoons of mixture onto sheet. Bake 8 to 9 minutes.

4. Cool 1 minute and transfer, top side down, to paper towels. Repeat, baking five at a time, until all mixture is used.

378

5. Melt chocolate and cocoa butter in top of a double boiler and dribble on cooled lace. Chill to harden chocolate.

Maple Syrup Oatmeal Cookies

Yield: About 3 dozen cookies

1 cup flour	½ cup shortening
¼ teaspoon salt	1 egg
1 teaspoon baking powder	¾ cup maple syrup
1 cup quick oats (uncooked)	½ teaspoon vanilla
½ cup chopped walnuts	

1. Preheat oven to 400 degrees.

2. Sift together flour, salt and baking powder. Add oats and nuts and mix well.

3. Cream shortening and egg until fluffy. Add maple syrup and vanilla; mix well. Stir in dry ingredients. Drop by teaspoonfuls, 2 inches apart, onto a greased baking sheet. Bake 8 to 12 minutes.

Maida Heatter's
Viennese Anise Cookies

Yield: About 6 dozen cookies

2 eggs	¼ teaspoon crushed anise
1 cup sugar	seed
1½ cups flour	1 teaspoon vanilla or
¼ teaspoon baking powder	¼ teaspoon grated
⅛ teaspoon salt	lemon rind

1. Break eggs into a measuring cup and add enough water to make ½ cup. In a small bowl, beat until thick and lemon colored. Gradually add sugar; beat until very thick, 15 to 20 minutes. Transfer to a large mixing bowl.

2. Sift together flour, baking powder and salt; sift, about ¼ cup at a time, over egg mixture. Fold in, along with crushed anise seed and vanilla, until well blended.

3. Cover baking sheets with baking pan liner paper (parchment paper).

4. Drop batter from a teaspoon, or use a pastry bag with ½-inch plain round tip to make cookies about 1½ inches in diameter. Let cookies stand overnight or 8 to 12 hours, uncovered. A hard crust will form on top.

5. Preheat oven to 350 degrees.

6. Bake cookies 7 or 8 minutes. Do not bake too dry. The cookies should have a soft base and a crisp top. They will puff up while baking. Cool cookies on rack and store in an airtight container.

Walnut Date Cookies

Yield: 4 dozen cookies

½ cup soft butter

¾ cup sugar

1 egg

½ teaspoon vanilla

1¼ cups flour

½ teaspoon salt

½ teaspoon baking soda

¾ cup coarsely chopped walnuts

¾ cup chopped dates

1 cup finely chopped walnuts

1. Preheat oven to 350 degrees.

2. Cream butter; add sugar and cream until light and fluffy. Stir in egg and vanilla.

3. Sift together flour, salt and soda. Add to butter mixture gradually. Stir in coarsely chopped walnuts and dates. Drop by teaspoonfuls into finely chopped walnuts and roll until coated.

4. Place on ungreased baking sheet and bake until lightly browned, 13 to 15 minutes.

Peanut Crunchies

Yield: 9 dozen cookies

1¼ cups granulated brown sugar

1 cup sugar

½ teaspoon salt

1 cup soft butter

¾ cup chunky peanut butter

2 eggs

2 cups flour

½ teaspoon baking soda

1 cup (6-ounce package) semisweet chocolate bits

1 cup salted peanuts

1. Preheat oven to 350 degrees.

2. Mix sugars, salt, butter and peanut butter thoroughly.

3. Beat eggs into mixture until light and fluffy.

4. Sift together flour and soda; gradually blend into sugar mixture. Stir in chocolate bits and peanuts.

5. Drop by teaspoonfuls, 2 inches apart, onto ungreased baking sheets. Bake 9 minutes or until light brown around edges. Cool on rack.

Chocolate-Dipped Mocha Cookies

Yield: 5 dozen cookies

½ cup shortening

½ cup soft butter

¾ cup sugar

1 egg

1 teaspoon vanilla

2¼ cups flour

2 tablespoons instant
coffee

½ teaspoon salt

¼ teaspoon baking powder

Chocolate Dip:

10 squares (10 ounces)
semisweet chocolate

1 ounce cocoa butter

1 cup finely chopped pecans

1. Preheat oven to 375 degrees.

2. Cream shortening, butter and sugar until very light and fluffy. Beat in egg and vanilla. Sift together flour, coffee, salt and baking powder. Stir into batter.

3. Using a cookie press fitted with a star plate (No. 2), and holding press in a semi-horizontal position, form 3-inch strips of dough on ungreased baking sheet. Bake 10 minutes or until browned. Cool on a rack.

4. Melt chocolate and cocoa butter slowly over hot, but not boiling, water. Dip both ends of cooled cookies into chocolate and then into nuts. Place on a rack to set. Refrigerate cookies (on rack) to hasten setting.

Sand Tarts

Yield: About 6 dozen cookies

2 cups flour

¼ teaspoon nutmeg

1 cup light brown sugar

⅔ cup soft butter

1 egg, lightly beaten

1 tablespoon milk

¼ cup sugar

¾ teaspoon cinnamon

1. Preheat oven to 400 degrees.

2. Place flour, nutmeg and brown sugar in a bowl and blend in butter until mixture resembles coarse oatmeal.

3. Mix to a dough with egg and milk. Shape into 1-inch balls; place on a lightly greased baking sheet 2 inches apart. Flatten each cooky with bottom of a glass. Sprinkle with sugar mixed with cinnamon. Bake 8 to 10 minutes.

Almond Cookies

Yield: About 5 dozen cookies

1 cup soft butter

1½ cups sifted con-
   fectioners' sugar

1 egg, lightly beaten

½ teaspoon almond extract

2½ cups flour

1 teaspoon cream of
   tartar

1 teaspoon salt

1 teaspoon baking soda

60 (approximately)
   blanched almonds

1. Blend butter with sugar. Using a wooden spoon, beat in egg and almond extract.

2. Sift together flour, cream of tartar, salt and soda. Stir into butter-sugar mixture. Cover and chill at least 1 hour.

3. Preheat oven to 375 degrees.

4. Using floured fingers, shape dough into about 60 small balls. Place balls on a baking sheet and press 1 almond into center of each. Bake 12 to 15 minutes.

Strawberry Sandwich Cookies

Yield: 16 squares

¼ cup soft butter

¼ cup shortening

½ cup sugar

1 egg

½ teaspoon vanilla

1½ cups flour

½ teaspoon salt

½ teaspoon baking powder

¾ cup strawberry preserves

1. Preheat oven to 400 degrees.

2. Blend butter, shortening, sugar, egg and vanilla in a bowl.

3. Combine flour, salt and baking powder. Add to butter mixture and mix well.

4. Spread half the dough in a buttered 8-inch square pan. Spread with preserves. Press remaining dough onto an 8-inch square of wax paper; place dough over preserves and peel off paper.

5. Bake 25 to 30 minutes. Cool and cut into 2-inch squares.

Honey Almond Squares

Yield: 6 to 10 dozen squares

3 eggs

1½ cups brown sugar

⅓ cup honey

1½ cups flour

1½ teaspoons baking powder

1 teaspoon salt

½ teaspoon cloves

¼ teaspoon nutmeg

2 tablespoons cocoa

½ cup finely ground
   blanched almonds

½ cup chopped
   blanched almonds

½ cup chopped mixed
   candied fruit

1½ cups confectioners' sugar

3 to 4 tablespoons cognac

1. Preheat oven to 350 degrees.

2. Beat eggs until foamy. Gradually beat in sugar until mixture is very thick. Beat in honey.

3. Sift flour with baking powder, salt, cloves and nutmeg. Mix in cocoa and ground almonds.

388

4. Fold flour mixture into egg mixture. Stir in chopped almonds and mixed fruits. Turn into greased jelly-roll pan, 15½ by 10½ inches. Bake 35 minutes.

5. Blend sugar with enough cognac to make a spreading consistency. Spread over hot cake. Cool and cut into 1- to 1½-inch squares.

389

Meringue Chocolate Nut Bars

Yield: 4 dozen bars

½ cup brown sugar	1 teaspoon vanilla
⅓ cup soft butter	¾ teaspoon salt
1⅓ cups flour	1 cup chopped nuts
½ teaspoon baking powder	1 cup (6-ounce package)
1 cup sugar	semisweet chocolate
2 eggs	bits

1. Preheat oven to 350 degrees.

2. Cream brown sugar and butter. Sift flour and baking powder and stir into creamed mixture. Press into greased 13-by-9-by-2-inch pan. Bake 8 minutes.

3. While batter is baking, prepare topping by beating the sugar, eggs, vanilla and salt until very thick and lemon colored. Fold in remaining ingredients gently and spread over cooked batter.

4. Bake 18 to 20 minutes longer. Cool and cut into bars.

Pies and Desserts

Lemon Tart

Yield: 6 servings

¾ cup flour	1 tart apple, peeled and
¼ teaspoon salt	finely grated
5 tablespoons soft butter	3 large lemons
2 to 3 tablespoons cold water	1 egg, lightly beaten
1 cup sugar	1 cup heavy cream
¾ cup whole almonds,	2 tablespoons confec-
blanched and finely	tioners' sugar
ground	

1. Preheat oven to 425 degrees.

2. Mix flour and salt in bowl. Blend in butter with fingertips or pastry blender. Using a fork, mix to a dough with water.

3. Roll dough on a lightly floured pastry cloth or board to a 9-inch circle. Fit into bottom of an 8-inch layer pan with removable bottom or a pie plate. Pastry will extend up sides. Prick pastry all over with fork.

4. Bake until firm but only very lightly browned, 10 to 15 minutes.

5. Combine sugar, ground almonds and apple. Spread over baked pastry, making sure the mixture goes all the way to the sides of pan.

6. Peel lemons; pull apart into segments, discarding membrane. Arrange lemon segments in cartwheel pattern over surface of almond mixture.

7. Beat egg and cream together lightly, just enough to mix. Pour over entire tart. Sprinkle with confectioners' sugar. Bake until set and lightly browned, about 30 minutes.

8. Let stand until lukewarm before serving. It is best served just warm but can be cooled and chilled.

Passover
Date and Apple Flan

Yield: 8 to 10 servings

Pastry:

1¼ cups matzoh meal

⅓ cup potato starch

3 tablespoons sugar

⅔ cup kosher-for-Passover
margarine

3 tablespoons (approximately) ice water

Filling:

2½ pounds tart apples
(about 6)

3 tablespoons sugar

3 tablespoons water

Grated rind and juice
of 1 lemon

1 cup chopped dates

1 large red eating apple

1. Combine matzoh meal, potato starch and sugar in a bowl. Blend in margarine with a pastry blender. Add ice water, 1 tablespoon at a time, until all particles are moistened. Wrap pastry in wax paper and chill about 1 hour.

2. Preheat oven to 350 degrees.

3. Roll dough between 2 sheets of wax paper into a round large enough to fit the bottom and sides of an ungreased 11½-inch flan ring set on a baking sheet.

4. Remove top sheet of wax paper, invert pastry into flan ring and remove second sheet. Press pastry into ring and trim edges. If it tears, patch it.

5. Bake about 15 minutes or until lightly browned. Cool.

6. Meanwhile, peel, core and slice tart apples and place in a saucepan with sugar, water and lemon rind. Cook, stirring frequently, until the mixture is very thick and smooth. There should be about 4 cups. Stir in dates and chill.

7. Just before serving, pour the apple filling into flan ring. Halve eating apple, core and cut into wafer-thin slices. Toss the slices in the lemon juice and arrange in a pinwheel pattern on top of the filling. Serve immediately.

Blueberry Pie
with Orange-Nut Crust

Yield: 8 servings

Crust:

- 2 cups flour
- ¼ teaspoon salt
- 2 teaspoons sugar
- ¾ cup shortening
- 1 teaspoon grated orange rind
- ⅓ cup finely chopped walnuts or pecans
- 5 tablespoons (approximately) ice water

Filling:

- 4 cups fresh blueberries
- 1 cup granulated sugar
- ¼ cup cornstarch
- ½ teaspoon nutmeg
- 2 tablespoons butter
- Confectioners' sugar

1. Mix flour, salt and sugar in a bowl. Cut in shortening with pastry blender. Add orange rind and nuts. Add water, 1 tablespoon at a time, mixing after each addition. Roll into a ball and refrigerate 1 hour before using.

2. Preheat oven to 375 degrees.

3. Roll out half the pastry and line a 9-inch pie pan.

4. Mix berries, granulated sugar, cornstarch and nutmeg. Pour mixture into pastry-lined pan. Dot with butter.

5. Roll out remaining pastry and cover top of pie. Moisten edges with water and seal. Cut a few slits in top to allow steam to escape.

6. Bake 1 hour. Remove from oven and cool on a rack. When cool, sprinkle with confectioners' sugar.

Deep-Dish Nectarine Pie

Yield: 6 to 8 servings

4 pounds ripe nectarines (about 16 medium)
1¼ cups sugar
¼ teaspoon salt
3 tablespoons quick-cooking tapioca
1 teaspoon vanilla
3 tablespoons butter
Pastry made with 1½ cups flour

1. Preheat oven to 425 degrees.

2. Skin and slice nectarines into a 10-by-6-by-2-inch baking dish. Combine sugar, salt, tapioca and vanilla and sprinkle over fruit. Dot with butter.

3. Roll pastry to a rectangle ⅛ inch thick and 2 inches larger than dish. Fit over casserole.

4. Trim crust; turn under, seal and flute edge. Make steam holes and bake 45 minutes or until the pastry is browned. Serve warm or cold.

Blueberry Velvet Custard Pie

Yield: 6 to 8 servings

4 eggs

⅔ cup sugar

½ teaspoon salt

½ teaspoon nutmeg

2⅔ cups milk

1 teaspoon vanilla

Unbaked 9-inch pie shell, chilled

1 cup blueberries, cleaned and drained

2 tablespoons orange juice

3 tablespoons confectioners' sugar

1. Preheat oven to 425 degrees.

2. Beat eggs until blended. Stir in sugar, salt, nutmeg, milk and vanilla. Pour into pie shell. Bake 15 minutes.

3. Reduce oven temperature to 350 degrees and bake 30 minutes longer, or until a knife inserted in filling about 1 inch from pastry edge comes out clean. Cool.

4. Mix blueberries, orange juice and confectioners' sugar; spoon over custard before serving.

399

Cream Plum Pie

Yield: 6 to 8 servings

Topping:
    4 cups pitted, quartered
        purple plums
    2½ cups sugar
    1 cup orange marmalade
    1 cup slivered blanched
        almonds
    2 tablespoons lemon juice

Filling:
    1 envelope unflavored
        gelatin
    ¼ cup cold water

½ cup sugar
¼ cup flour
½ teaspoon salt
2 cups milk, scalded
3 egg yolks, lightly
    beaten
2 tablespoons butter
3 tablespoons cognac
½ cup heavy cream,
    whipped
Baked 9- or 10-inch pie
    shell, cooled

1. Preheat oven to 325 degrees.

2. Mix plums with sugar. Place in a shallow roasting pan and cover with aluminum foil.

3. Bake until mixture starts to thicken, about 1 hour. Stir in marmalade, almonds and lemon juice. Chill.

4. Soften gelatin in cold water.

5. Mix together sugar, flour and salt; gradually stir in milk. Pour mixture into top of double boiler and heat, stirring, over direct heat until mixture thickens. Cook, covered, over boiling water 10 minutes.

6. Stir some of hot mixture into egg yolks, return to pan and cook until thickened, about 5 minutes. Remove from heat. Add butter and gelatin and mix well. Cool. Add cognac.

7. Fold in whipped cream and pour into pie shell. Chill.

8. Use plum topping as a border or all over the pie when it is served. Extra topping can be used as a conserve.

Kentucky Lemon Pie

Yield: 8 to 10 servings

Filling:

6 eggs

1½ cups light corn syrup

¾ cup sugar

1 teaspoon cornstarch

½ cup lemon juice

Grated rind of 1 lemon

1 teaspoon melted butter

Unbaked 10-inch pie
shell, with stand-up
edge, chilled

Meringue:

4 egg whites, at room
temperature

¼ teaspoon cream of
tartar

4 tablespoons confec-
tioners' sugar

1. Preheat oven to 375 degrees.

2. Beat eggs with a rotary beater until well mixed. Add syrup
and continue beating.

3. Mix sugar and cornstarch. Beat into egg mixture.

4. Add lemon juice, rind and butter. Beat until thoroughly mixed.

5. Pour carefully into chilled pie shell. Bake 15 minutes. Reduce oven temperature to 300 degrees; bake 45 minutes longer or until set. Cool and chill.

6. To prepare meringue, beat egg whites until frothy. Add cream of tartar and continue beating until stiff. Add sugar, 1 tablespoon at a time, beating well after each addition.

7. When ready to top the pie with meringue, preheat oven to 350 degrees. Spread meringue over filling so meringue touches the pastry edge all around. Leave surface rough. Bake 10 minutes, until meringue is lightly browned. Cool and chill again before serving.

Chocolate-Butterscotch Pie

Yield: 8 servings

3 cups light brown sugar

½ cup butter

3 eggs

1 teaspoon vanilla

½ cup light cream

1 ounce unsweetened chocolate, melted

Unbaked 9-inch pie shell, with stand-up edge, chilled

1 cup sweetened heavy cream, whipped

Chocolate shavings

1. Preheat oven to 350 degrees.

2. Beat sugar and butter together until creamy. Beat in eggs, one at a time. Add vanilla.

3. Beat in light cream; add chocolate and beat to mix completely. Pour into pie shell and bake 30 minutes. Reduce heat to 300 degrees and continue to bake 50 minutes longer or until set. Cool. Decorate with whipped cream and chocolate shavings. The pie falls as it cools.

404

Raisin Pie

Yield: 6 to 8 servings

1 cup white corn syrup	¾ teaspoon allspice
3 large eggs, lightly beaten	¼ teaspoon nutmeg
½ cup sugar	1 cup raisins, plumped
2 tablespoons butter	¼ cup chopped pecans
¼ teaspoon salt	or walnuts
½ teaspoon grated lemon	Unbaked 9-inch pie shell,
rind	chilled

1. Preheat oven to 425 degrees.

2. Combine syrup, eggs, sugar, butter, salt, lemon rind, allspice and nutmeg. Mix well. Add raisins and nuts and pour into pie shell.

3. Bake 10 minutes. Reduce heat to 350 degrees and bake 30 to 35 minutes longer. Filling solidifies further on cooling.

Marmalade Pie

Yield: 8 servings

2 medium-size oranges	¼ cup soft butter
1¼ cups sugar	3 eggs
Juice of ½ lemon	2 tablespoons Grand
½ cup plus 1 teaspoon	Marnier
water	Pastry for 2-crust
2½ tablespoons cornstarch	9-inch pie

1. Wash and dry oranges. Peel off paper-thin, bright part of skin with a potato peeler and chop very finely.

2. Separate oranges into sections. Put sections in a saucepan and squeeze any extra juice that remains in membranes into pan. Discard membrane. Add chopped rind, ¼ cup sugar, lemon juice and ½ cup water to saucepan. Bring to a boil; boil gently 15 minutes, uncovered. Cool to room temperature.

3. Preheat oven to 425 degrees.

4. Place remaining sugar in a mixing bowl with cornstarch and mix. Add butter and beat until smooth and fluffy. Beat in eggs, one at a time, reserving 1 teaspoon of a yolk.

5. Fold in cooled marmalade mixture and the Grand Marnier. Pour into a 9-inch pie pan lined with pastry.

6. Roll remaining pastry into strips and arrange in a lattice pattern over top. Combine reserved egg yolk with teaspoon of water and brush over pastry.

7. Bake 10 minutes. Reduce oven temperature to 350 degrees; bake 30 to 40 minutes longer until pie is set. Cool.

Note: This pie may be served with a whipped cream made by whipping 1 cup heavy cream with 2 tablespoons confectioners' sugar and 2 teaspoons grated orange rind.

Almond Pie

Yield: 8 servings

3 eggs, lightly beaten

1 cup dark corn syrup

1 cup brown sugar

3 tablespoons butter,
   melted

1 teaspoon vanilla

⅛ teaspoon salt

Unbaked 9-inch pie shell,
   chilled

1 cup blanched almonds

1. Preheat oven to 350 degrees.

2. Mix eggs, syrup, sugar, butter, vanilla and salt. Turn into pie shell and sprinkle almonds over the top.

3. Bake until firm, about 1 hour. If desired, serve sprinkled with confectioners' sugar.

Chocolate Walnut Pie

Yield: 6 to 8 servings

4 tablespoons butter

1 cup sugar

½ cup flour

2 eggs, lightly beaten

1 cup broken walnut meats

1 cup semisweet chocolate
bits

1 teaspoon vanilla

Unbaked 8-inch pie shell,
chilled

1. Preheat oven to 350 degrees.

2. Melt butter, then set aside to cool slightly.

3. Sift sugar and flour into a mixing bowl. Stir in eggs, then add butter. Stir in walnuts, chocolate bits and vanilla.

4. Pour mixture into pie shell and bake until filling is fairly firm, ½ hour or longer.

Peanut Pie

Yield: 6 servings

2 eggs

1 cup dark corn syrup

1 cup sugar

1 teaspoon vanilla

1 cup salted peanuts

2 tablespoons butter

Unbaked 9-inch pie shell, chilled

1. Preheat oven to 350 degrees.

2. In a mixing bowl, combine eggs, corn syrup, sugar and vanilla. Stir in peanuts and scrape mixture into pie shell. Dot with butter and bake 45 to 50 minutes or until set.

Maple Chiffon Pie

Yield: 6 servings

1 envelope unflavored
    gelatin
3 tablespoons cold water
½ cup milk
½ cup maple syrup
⅓ teaspoon salt

2 eggs, separated
1 cup heavy cream, whipped
1 teaspoon vanilla
    Baked 9-inch pie shell,
    cooled

1. Soften gelatin in cold water.

2. Heat milk, syrup and salt in top of double boiler. Lightly beat egg yolks and spoon a little of hot milk mixture into them, beating well. Return to pan and cook until thick. Remove from heat and stir in softened gelatin until it dissolves. Cool and chill until mixture begins to set.

3. Beat whites until stiff but not dry; fold into thickening gelatin mixture. Fold in half the whipped cream and the vanilla. Pour into pie shell. Chill. Top with whipped cream.

411

Coffee
Banana Cream Pie

Yield: 6 to 8 servings

½ cup sugar

5 tablespoons flour

¼ teaspoon salt

1 cup evaporated milk

1 cup strong coffee

2 egg yolks, lightly beaten

1 tablespoon butter

½ teaspoon vanilla

3 ripe bananas, sliced

Baked 9-inch pie shell, cooled

Whipped cream

1. Combine sugar, flour and salt in top of a double boiler. Combine evaporated milk and coffee and add slowly to sugar mixture. Cook, stirring, over boiling water until thick. Cook 10 minutes longer, stirring occasionally.

2. Stir a small amount of hot mixture into yolks; then pour yolks into remaining hot mixture while beating vigorously. Cook, stirring, 1 minute longer. Remove from heat; stir in butter and vanilla. Cool.

3. Alternate layers of banana slices and filling in pie shell. Chill. Top with whipped cream and garnish with slices of banana.

Bourbon Pie

Yield: 6 to 8 servings

5 egg yolks
¾ cup sugar
1 envelope unflavored gelatin
¼ cup water
⅓ cup bourbon or rum

2 cups heavy cream, whipped
Baked 9-inch pie shell, cooled
½ square unsweetened chocolate, shaved

1. Beat egg yolks and gradually add sugar. Beat constantly until mixture is light yellow and thick.

2. Soften gelatin in water and heat over boiling water until dissolved. Add to yolk mixture. Mix well and add bourbon.

3. Fold in whipped cream and pour into pie shell. Sprinkle with chocolate shavings. Chill at least 6 hours.

Blueberry Cheese Pie

Yield: 6 to 8 servings

2 tablespoons cold water

2 tablespoons lemon juice

1 envelope unflavored
gelatin

½ cup milk, scalded

2 egg yolks

⅓ cup sugar

2 cups creamed cottage
cheese

9-inch graham cracker
crust, chilled

½ cup currant jelly

1 pint blueberries

1. Place cold water, lemon juice and gelatin in blender container. Cover and blend at low speed. Add hot milk. If gelatin granules cling to container, push down with rubber spatula.

2. When gelatin is dissolved, turn control to high speed; add egg yolks, sugar and cottage cheese. Blend until smooth.

3. Pour into prepared crust. Chill until firm, about 2 hours. Melt currant jelly, stir smooth and let cool. Stir berries into cooled jelly until coated. Spoon over pie. Chill.

Rhubarb-Strawberry Delight

Yield: 6 servings

3 cups (approximately)
  sliced fresh strawberries

1 cup (approximately)
  diced, cooked sweetened
  rhubarb

1 envelope unflavored
  gelatin

¾ cup cold dry white wine

½ cup boiling water

½ cup sugar

2 egg whites

⅛ teaspoon salt

¼ teaspoon almond extract

1. Puree 1 cup strawberries to make ½ cup pulp; set aside. Puree rhubarb to make ½ cup pulp; set aside.

2. Soften gelatin in ¼ cup wine. Add water; stir to dissolve. Add remaining wine and sugar and stir to dissolve. Cool until mixture thickens. Fold in pulps; beat until foamy.

3. Beat egg whites until stiff but not dry. Fold whites, salt and extract into fruit mixture. Spoon into sherbet glasses or individual molds. Serve with remaining berries.

415

Valentine
Strawberry Soufflés

Yield: 2 servings

1½ teaspoons unflavored
    gelatin
2 tablespoons water
2 eggs, separated
⅓ cup sugar
⅛ teaspoon salt

1 package (10 ounces)
    frozen sliced straw-
    berries
½ cup heavy cream,
    whipped
Red food coloring
    (optional)

1. Fit 2 individual soufflé dishes with lightly oiled foil collars that extend 1½ inches above rims.

2. Soak gelatin in water.

3. Place egg yolks and ¼ cup sugar in top of a small double boiler. Add salt and beat lightly to mix. Cook over barely simmering water, stirring, until mixture thickens. Do not boil mixture.

416

4. Heat gelatin just long enough to dissolve and add to egg yolk mixture.

5. Puree strawberries in an electric blender or a sieve. Measure ½ cup. (Remaining puree can be used as an ice cream topping.) Fold puree into egg yolk mixture and cool until mixture begins to thicken slightly.

6. Beat egg whites until frothy. Gradually add remaining sugar, continuing to beat until stiff but not dry. Fold into strawberry mixture. Add a few drops of red coloring, if desired.

7. Fold in whipped cream, reserving a little for decorating. Spoon into dishes and chill several hours. Remove collars and decorate with whipped cream.

Orange Bavarian Cream

Yield: 6 servings

1 envelope unflavored gelatin

¼ cup cold water

½ cup plus 2 tablespoons unstrained orange juice

½ teaspoon grated orange rind

2 tablespoons lemon juice

⅓ cup sugar

¼ teaspoon salt

2 tablespoons orange-flavored liqueur, cognac or rum

1 cup heavy cream, whipped

3 cups fresh orange sections

1. Soften gelatin in water. Heat orange juice and rind, lemon juice, sugar and salt. Add gelatin and stir to dissolve.

2. Chill until consistency of unbeaten egg whites. Fold in liqueur, cream and 1 cup orange sections, drained and diced. Pour into a 1-quart mold and chill until firm.

3. Unmold and garnish with reserved orange sections.

Grapefruit Delight

Yield: 6 servings

1 envelope unflavored
  gelatin
¼ cup water
1 cup fresh grapefruit juice
6 tablespoons sugar

1 cup fresh grapefruit
  sections
2 egg whites
½ teaspoon vanilla
  Grapefruit sections for
  garnish

1. Soften gelatin in water. Place over hot water until dissolved.

2. Combine grapefruit juice and 4 tablespoons sugar and stir until sugar is dissolved. Add gelatin mixture.

3. Chill until mixture starts to thicken. Stir in grapefruit.

4. Beat egg whites until stiff. Beat in remaining sugar and add vanilla; fold into gelatin mixture. Pour into oiled 1-quart mold. Chill until firm. Unmold and decorate with grapefruit sections.

419

Strawberry-Pineapple Rice

Yield: 8 servings

1½ cups milk
2 tablespoons sugar
½ cup rice
1½ teaspoons unflavored
   gelatin
1 tablespoon cold water
1 pineapple, peeled, cored
   and cubed

2 crisp apples, peeled,
   cored and diced
½ cup seedless grapes
1 cup fresh strawberries
2 tablespoons Grand
   Marnier
1 cup heavy cream,
   whipped

1. Combine milk, sugar and rice in top of a double boiler. Bring to boil over direct heat; place over boiling water. Cover and cook 20 minutes or until rice is tender. Stir twice. Soften gelatin in water. Stir into rice. Chill.

2. Cover pineapple cubes with boiling water; allow to stand 5 minutes; drain.

3. Combine pineapple cubes with other fruits, reserving a few pieces of each for garnish, and sprinkle with liqueur. Chill.

4. Fold fruits, liqueur and whipped cream into rice. Spoon into parfait glasses or a large serving bowl. Garnish with reserved fruits.

Chocolate Macaroon Dessert

Yield: 10 or more servings

½ pound blanched almonds

¼ cup bourbon or rum

2 cups crumbled
  macaroons

6 tablespoons butter

½ pound confectioners'
  sugar

5 eggs, separated

2 squares (1 ounce each)
  semisweet chocolate

3 tablespoons water

½ teaspoon vanilla

18 ladyfingers

1 pint heavy cream,
  sweetened and
  whipped

1. Preheat oven to 350 degrees.

2. Scatter almonds over a baking sheet and bake 10 minutes or until almonds are toasted. Stir occasionally so that they toast evenly. Let almonds cool. Reserve ⅛ cup of almonds for garnish. Chop remaining almonds.

3. Pour whiskey or rum over macaroons. Set aside.

4. Place butter in mixing bowl and beat with an electric mixer. Beat in sugar.

5. Beat egg yolks until lemon colored and beat into butter-sugar mixture.

6. Combine chocolate with water, melt over low heat and add to butter mixture. Beat until blended. Stir in almonds and vanilla. Beat egg whites until stiff. Fold into the chocolate mixture.

7. Line bottom and sides of a 1½-quart crystal serving bowl with ladyfinger halves, split side in. Add a thin layer of crumbled macaroons and a layer of chocolate batter. Continue making alternate layers of macaroons and chocolate. Cover and refrigerate overnight.

8. Spoon whipped cream on top of cake and garnish with reserved almonds.

Chocolate Mousse

Yield: 8 servings

6 ounces (6 squares) semisweet chocolate

4 tablespoons water

4 eggs, separated

¾ cup plus 1 tablespoon sugar

¼ cup Grand Marnier

10 tablespoons soft butter

⅛ teaspoon salt

1 cup heavy cream,
   whipped

1. Melt chocolate with water in top of a double boiler over hot, but not boiling, water. Mix egg yolks in a small sauce-pan with ¾ cup sugar. Heat gently, stirring, until mixture thickens; do not boil. Off heat, immediately add liqueur.

2. Beat butter into chocolate mixture; when smooth, add to cooked yolks. Fold in whipped cream.

3. Beat egg whites with remaining tablespoon sugar until stiff but not dry. Fold into chocolate mixture. Pour into individual serving dishes or a large bowl and chill well.

Cantaloupe Ice Cream

Yield: 10 to 12 servings

1 quart vanilla ice cream
2 cups peeled, mashed fresh
    cantaloupe
1 cup heavy cream, whipped

1 tablespoon sugar
Melon balls and mint
    sprigs

1. Let ice cream stand at room temperature until soft enough to stir. Blend in cantaloupe. Spoon into a 6-cup mold. Freeze.

2. About an hour before serving, quickly dip mold into hot water and turn out onto a serving plate. Place in freezer again for a few minutes to harden surface.

3. Frost mold or decorate with whipped cream sweetened with sugar. Return to freezer until serving time. Garnish with melon balls and mint sprigs.

Choco-Orange Ice

Yield: 1 quart

2 teaspoons unflavored
   gelatin
3½ cups plus 2 table-
   spoons water
2 cups sugar
   Grated rind of 2 large
   oranges

4 ounces (4 squares)
   unsweetened chocolate
1 teaspoon vanilla
½ cup fresh orange juice

1. Soften gelatin in 2 tablespoons water.

2. Combine remaining water with sugar in a small saucepan. Heat slowly and stir until sugar is dissolved. Increase heat and boil rapidly 5 minutes without stirring. Remove from heat and stir in gelatin and rind. Cool to lukewarm.

3. Melt chocolate over hot, but not boiling, water in double boiler; cool slightly. Place warm chocolate in a bowl and gradually beat in warm sugar syrup with rotary beater.

426

4. Add vanilla and juice and pour into a freezing tray. Cover with foil and freeze until frozen around edges and mushy in middle.

5. Beat until smooth and refreeze. Remove from refrigerator 15 minutes before serving.

Bananas Flambées

Yield: 6 servings

6 ripe bananas, sliced on
   the bias
Juice of ½ lemon
1 cup brown sugar

½ cup butter
½ teaspoon cinnamon
¼ cup cognac
Vanilla ice cream

1. Brush bananas with lemon juice. Melt sugar and butter in a flat chafing dish. Add bananas and cook until just tender.

2. Sprinkle bananas with cinnamon. Warm cognac and add. Ignite; pour flaming banana mixture over ice cream balls.

Nectarine Sherbet

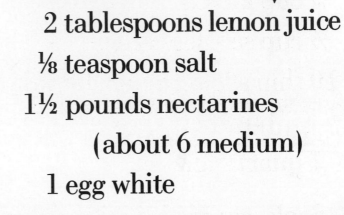

Yield: About 3 pints

1 envelope unflavored gelatin	2 tablespoons lemon juice
¼ cup cold water	⅛ teaspoon salt
1 cup sugar	1½ pounds nectarines (about 6 medium)
1 cup milk	1 egg white

1. Soften gelatin in cold water. Heat until gelatin is dissolved. Combine sugar, milk, lemon juice, salt and gelatin.

2. Peel and slice nectarines; puree in blender and add to gelatin mixture. Pour into a freezing tray.

3. Freeze until almost firm. Turn into mixing bowl, add egg white and beat with rotary or electric beater until smooth and fluffy. Freeze in 2 trays until firm and ready to serve. Soften slightly before serving.

Bread and Butter Pudding

Yield: 10 servings

½ cup mixed candied fruit

¼ cup kirsch

½ cup seedless raisins

10 thin slices French bread,
    buttered

1 quart milk

1 cup cream

1 cup sugar

5 whole eggs

4 egg yolks

1 teaspoon vanilla

Confectioners' sugar

1. Soak candied fruit in kirsch; set aside. Cover raisins with boiling water. Let stand 5 minutes; drain.

2. Preheat oven to 375 degrees.

3. Bring milk and cream to a boil; stir in sugar. Stir hot mixture into beaten eggs and yolks. Add vanilla.

4. Place candied fruit, kirsch and bread in buttered 2-quart baking dish. Strain custard over. Set dish in pan of boiling water. Bake 45 minutes or until set.

5. Sprinkle with confectioners' sugar and glaze under broiler.

Apple Crisp

Yield: 6 servings

7 or 8 medium-size tart
    cooking apples
1 cup light brown sugar
½ teaspoon cinnamon
⅛ teaspoon nutmeg
1 tablespoon lemon juice

Grated rind of 1 orange
2 tablespoons orange juice
¾ cup flour
¼ teaspoon salt
6 tablespoons soft butter

1. Preheat oven to 375 degrees.

2. Peel, core and slice apples into a greased 9-inch deep-dish pie pan or a 1-quart shallow casserole. Mix ½ cup sugar with cinnamon and nutmeg and sprinkle over apples. Add lemon juice, orange rind and juice.

3. In a small bowl, mix together flour, salt and remaining sugar. Cut in butter and sprinkle mixture over apples. Bake 45 minutes or until apples are tender and top is browned.

Apple Rum Float

Yield: 6 servings

2 cups applesauce	2 teaspoons cinnamon
1 cup light brown sugar	1 teaspoon nutmeg
1 cup broken pecans	⅛ teaspoon allspice
1 cup seedless raisins	4 egg whites
⅔ cup dark rum	½ cup granulated sugar

1. Preheat oven to 325 degrees.

2. Combine applesauce, brown sugar, pecans, raisins, rum and spices in a saucepan. Bring to a boil. Spoon into a 6-cup casserole.

3. Beat egg whites stiff and gradually beat in granulated sugar. Pile lightly on top of pudding in casserole. Bake 15 to 20 minutes or until meringue is a delicate brown. Serve at once.

Apple Pancake

Yield: 6 servings

1 pound tart apples (3 or 4)

10 tablespoons melted butter

10 tablespoons sugar

¼ teaspoon cinnamon

⅛ teaspoon nutmeg

½ teaspoon grated lemon rind

2 eggs, beaten

½ cup milk

½ cup flour

¼ teaspoon salt

1. Preheat oven to 450 degrees.

2. Pare, core and cut apples into thin slices. Cook slowly in a large skillet with 5 tablespoons butter for 5 minutes.

3. Combine 5 tablespoons sugar with cinnamon, nutmeg and lemon rind and add to apples. Cover and cook over low heat 10 minutes or until apples are crisp-tender. Cool to lukewarm.

4. Make a batter by beating eggs with milk, flour and salt.

5. Heat 1 tablespoon of remaining butter in a heavy ovenproof skillet. Pour batter into pan and bake 15 minutes, pricking the batter after about 3 minutes, when it puffs up, and several times as it rises again. Reduce oven temperature to 350 degrees; bake 10 minutes longer or until crisp and golden. Batter will form a crisp shell.

6. Remove from oven. Pour 2 tablespoons butter over shell and sprinkle with half the remaining sugar. Place apple mixture over half the surface, fold like an omelet and tip onto a warm platter. Sprinkle pancake with remaining butter and sugar.

Fresh Blueberry Buckle

Yield: 6 to 8 servings

½ cup soft butter

1 cup sugar

1 egg

½ teaspoon vanilla

1⅓ cups flour

1 teaspoon baking powder

¼ teaspoon salt

⅓ cup milk

2 cups fresh blueberries

½ teaspoon ground cardamom

¼ teaspoon nutmeg

Sweetened whipped cream

1. Preheat oven to 375 degrees.

2. Cream together half the butter and half the sugar. Beat in egg and vanilla.

3. Sift together 1 cup flour, baking powder and salt. Add alternately with milk to creamed mixture starting and ending with dry ingredients. Pour into a greased 9-inch square baking dish. Top with blueberries.

4. Combine remaining sugar and flour, cardamom and nutmeg. Using a pastry blender, cut in remaining butter until texture is like coarse cornmeal. Sprinkle over blueberries.

5. Bake 40 to 45 minutes. Cool slightly before serving with sweetened whipped cream.

INDEX

Alaska king crab soufflé, 238
Almond
    cookies, 386
    cream cake, 360
    honey squares, 388
    pie, 408
Amico, Mrs. Joseph, roast duck
    with sour cherries, 166
Anchovy
    and tomato canapés, 41
    butter, 245
Angels on horseback, 37
Anise cookies, Viennese,
    Maida Heatter's, 380
Appetizer(s)
    angels on horseback, 37
    baked oysters, 47
    briks, 26
    cheese crisps, 22
    cherry soup with farina,
        cold, 78
    chicken liver
        -champagne pâté, 15
        strudel slices, 28
    chicken pâté loaf, 16
    cocktail
        meat balls, 34
        wafers, 23
    crab (meat), 32
        -stuffed tomatoes, 21
        vinaigrette, 46
    creamed oysters in
        barquettes, 48
    dolmadakia, 44

Appetizer(s) *(cont.)*
    egg and endive, 20
    gefilte fish crescents, 24
    guacamole, 12
    ham cornets, 42
    laban, 14
    marinated salmon, 18
    miniature drumsticks, 36
    pissaladière Provençale, 336
    salmon sour cream dip, 13
    sea food
        canapés, 40
        mold, 102
    seviche, 39
    shrimp
        quiches, individual, 30
        tarragon, 50
    tomato and anchovy
        canapés, 41
    tuna-stuffed eggs, 19
    tuna-stuffed mushrooms, 38
Apple
    and date flan, Passover, 394
    cake, Mrs. Davis', 370
    crisp, 430
    marmalade, 319
    muffins, 347
    pancake, 432
    rum float, 431
    soup, Hungarian, 80
Arroz con gandules, 266
Artichoke fritters, 296
Asparagus and sole, 95
Aspic, shrimp and salmon, 126

Babka, 340
Bacon and cheese pudding, 242

Baked
    beans, 273
    butter beans with pears, 297
    cauliflower mayonnaise, 302
    oysters, 47
    vegetables country-style, 310
    wild rice with carrots, 270
Banana(s)
    cream coffee pie, 412
    flambées, 427
    -sour cream coffeecake, 358
Barbecue(d)
    chicken, 132
    halibut steaks, 88
    oven-, spareribs, 216
    steak, Korean, 187
Barley casserole, 271
Basic sweet dough, 342
Bass
    rice-stuffed, 82
    striped, poached, 84
Bavarian cream, orange, 418
Bean(s)
    baked, 273
    butter, baked, with pears, 297
    country-style, 276
    frijoles, 272
    green, with mustard, 298
    Mexican, 272
    -olive soup, 60
    pinto, pot, 274
    rarebit, 239
    rice and lentil casserole, 264
Beef
    boiled, 190
    bul kogi, 187
    caraway short ribs, 189

438

439

444

Stuffed *(cont.)*
  mussels, 106
  shrimp, crab-stuffed, 116
  tomatoes, crab-stuffed, 21
  turkey breast, 160
Sweet dough, basic, 342
Swordfish
  à l'Espagnole, 99
  shish, 98

Tarragon
  lamb chops with, 204
  shrimp, 50
Tart, lemon, 392
Tollgate Farm meat balls and
    sauerkraut, 194
Tomato(es)
  and anchovy canapés, 41
  and zucchini salad, 295
  crab-stuffed, 21
  marinated, 294
  marmalade, 321
  sauce, fresh, 247
  shells, eggs in, 232
  with salad Russe, 293
Tongue
  loaf, jellied, 224
  sauce (caper or
    horseradish), 257
Tournedos, 184
Trout
  meunière, 100
  sauce (mustard), 248

Tuna
  briks, 26
  soup with capers, 72
  stuffed
    eggs, 19
    mushrooms, 38
Turkey
  breast, stuffed, 160
  curried, 159
Turnip soup, cold cream of, 75

Valentine strawberry
    soufflés, 416
Veal
  birds, 218
  Hungarian goulash, 180
  kidneys with celery, 228
  loaf, 223
  Madelon, Eleanor's, 222
  saltimbocca, 217
  sauces for
    belle aurore, 256
    mushroom, 249
    paprika, 250
    paprika sour cream,
     258
  stuffed breast of, 220
Vegetable(s). *See also specific vegetable*
  and chicken curry, 136
  and rice soup, 58
  baked, country-style, 310
  salad, Malagasy, 288

Vegetable(s) *(cont.)*
  sauces for
    cream cheese, 243
    hollandaise, 251
    lemon butter, 252
    quick hollandaise, 252
Venison stew, 172
Vichyssoise piquante, 76
Viennese anise cookies,
    Maida Heatter's, 380
Vivian's chocolate lace, 378

Walnut
  cake, 352
  chocolate pie, 409
  date cookies, 382
Watercress
  endive and beets, 290
  soup, cream of, 62
Whole wheat bread, 330
Wild rice
  baked, with carrots, 270
  casserole, 269
Winter chutney, 325

Yogurt
  and cucumber soup, 74
  coffeecake, 364
  laban, 14

Zucchini
  and tomato salad, 295
  Smetana, 312

446

CDEFGH